T0195009

The
Hidden Side
of Life

*The Effects
of Unseen
Energies*

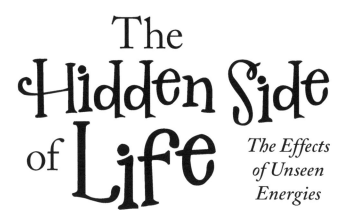

JAMES W. PETERSON

iUniverse®

THE HIDDEN SIDE OF LIFE
THE EFFECTS OF UNSEEN ENERGIES

iUniverse books may be ordered through booksellers or by contacting:

iUniverse
1663 Liberty Drive
Bloomington, IN 47403
www.iuniverse.com
844-349-9409

ISBN: 978-1-6632-3885-6 (sc)
ISBN: 978-1-6632-3884-9 (e)

Library of Congress Control Number: 2022907708

Print information available on the last page.

iUniverse rev. date: 05/26/2022

For M. S. Irani

CONTENTS

ACKNOWLEDGMENTS

There are many people who helped to bring this book into print. My wife, Hana, was a great help. She helped me find quiet time to write, even on vacations. And anecdotes from her own spiritual life enrich the text of several sections. She also typed many of the chapters.

I wish to also thank my editor, Rachel Dacus, who worked hard to help me improve the manuscript and put it into tip-top shape. Allan Francke was another editor who saved the day in the final stages of the book. He retyped and re-edited several chapters that were mysteriously lost in my computer.

Two others have found their way into my book. My dear old Gnostic friend, Bishop Stephan Hoeller, kindly penned the foreword for this volume. And my equally dear son, Blake Peterson, executed the brilliant painting on the cover.

Finally, I wish to thank my spiritual teachers, Murshid James MacKie and Murshida Carol Weyland Conner, for encouraging me and inspiring me to put pen to paper and explore the hidden side of life.

FOREWORD

Human consciousness has a great desire to search for that which is hidden. The great mystery writers, such as Conan Doyle and Rex Stout, would have remained unknown had it not been for their talent in discovering the hidden side of the lives and deeds of the individuals (often of criminal disposition) in their tales. In addition to the hidden side of humans, there was often recognized a realm of focus and beings of a preternatural character that together constituted the hidden side of life.

Engaged in interaction with this hidden side of existence, we find a vast panorama of shamans, prophets, seers, and magic practitioners who often become the informants of ordinary folk regarding the presence of the hidden side of life. The Latin word for "hidden" is *occult*, and in nineteenth-century thinking and parlance, the generic term "occultism" was often applied to the field of the study and observation of the hidden side of things.

Over the last century and a half, people with a fervent interest in science often combined this intellectual study with their secret interest of the occult and created a hybrid, named occult science.

Be that as it may, the hidden side of life is a subject of abiding interest among humans. As a result, our knowledge of things previously hidden has increased to a great degree. From the hidden side of the interior of the atom, to the hidden side of the vast distance of outer space, we have uncovered much that without our skills would have remained hidden. At the same time, we need to admit that the subjects whose hidden side we have discovered were external to our internal nature, to our minds. Curiously, our search for the hidden side of life has become an exercise in extroversion, in the outward direction of our consciousness.

Consciousness itself is a mysterious component of life. It is complemented by what psychology calls the unconscious. Civilization, especially for the last two hundred years or so, has come to overvalue the conscious mind, while leaving the unconscious in the dark. Yet there appears to be a law of the soul or mind that declares that the hidden must manifest. The extroversion of consciousness is able to proceed outward only for so long, until it meets an impassable barrier that forces it to turn toward the interior mystery.

The author of the present work may be described as an explorer of the soul-landscape of humanity. He spent much of his adult life as a teacher of children, following the enlightened Waldorf Method of education. He has now expanded the scope of his inquiry to include subjects that concern young and old. The subjects he addresses are numerous and of manifold interest. He delves into the subject of water and then gazes into the heavens by glancing at astrology; from there, he proceeds to medicine, gardening, and child-rearing. Of spiritual fields of interest, he writes of meditation, the power of thought, reincarnation, and the mysteries of the mineral kingdom. As his first book, *The Secret Life of Kids,* was a work of research into the inner experiences of childhood, so this work draws on his own life experiences as enriched by insights gained in the teachings of theosophy and culminating in the contemporary Sufism of the noted master, Meher Baba.

This is a book that is practical as well as theoretical, studious as well as intuitive, while it reflects the personal experiences and experientially gained insights of a man in whom learning and reflection, wisdom and practicality, intuition and humor have reached a happy conjunction.

To the reader, I wish an inspiring and informative time while reading this book.

Dr. Stephan A. Hoeller
Author of *The Gnostic Jung*

INTRODUCTION

What is reality? It's a subtle energy. We call it
wind. Wind means movement, energy.
—His Holiness, the Dalai Lama

"I suggest that you might wear a red robe when you're sick," my first Sufi teacher once said. "The color red attracts energies that can aid in healing."

In 1970, at the age of twenty-one, this was one of the first instances when I learned how to integrate a practical understanding of the effects of unseen energies into a spiritually oriented life. As a college student in Berkeley, I had also experienced the unpleasant drug atmosphere of Telegraph Avenue, as well as the uplifting light generated by the practice of meditation. So, early in my spiritual quest, the hidden side of life was already quite apparent to me. Every day, over these last forty-five years, the presence in my life of myriad unseen forces has been for me both obvious and fascinating. In this book, I would like to share some of what I've learned.

Albert Einstein, who popularized the idea that energy is everywhere, once said, "Something deeply hidden has to be behind things." I would like to explore with you this hidden side of things.

The well-known spiritual figure from South India, Sri Aurobindo Ghose, once wrote, "Anyone with some intelligence and power of observation who lives more in an inward consciousness can see the play of invisible forces at every step which act on men and bring about events without their knowing about the instrumentation.... One becomes conscious of these invisible forces and can also profit by them or use and direct them" (Sri Aurobindo, *Letters on Yoga*, p 78). "Profiting," in my view, means living a happier, more satisfying life.

Explaining and expanding on the words of an authoritative spiritual figure such as Sri Aurobindo, however, is not the scheme of this book. I'm going to rely primarily on one authority: myself. My first book, *The Secret Life of Kids*, was research oriented. I collected data and explained and supported the data by other relevant research and authoritative theories of scientists.

After almost fifty years of study, meditation, and trying to tread the spiritual path, I wish to share my own personal experiences and personal knowing. An abbreviation commonly used on the internet is IMHO: "in my humble opinion." That will be the living backdrop of this book: my opinion. The background of my own lifelong spiritual quest will therefore come up frequently in the following chapters. My life experience, naturally, has forged my personal opinions. Here is a small introduction to my spiritual orientation.

I was raised in the Methodist church. In fact, both my grandfathers were ministers. However, my parents and siblings took no real interest in spiritual matters. Even though my parents sent my brothers and me to Sunday school, a feeling of parental duty was behind it, rather than the view of guiding us toward spiritual truth.

This guidance for me came when I discovered the Theosophical Society in nearby Wheaton, Illinois. I became a member in March of 1967, when I turned eighteen. The Theosophical Society is a worldwide organization dedicated to the exploration of spiritual principles common to every religious tradition. It was from my first theosophical mentor that I learned of the existence of spiritual masters, the inner planes of consciousness, reincarnation, and karma.

With this new esoteric worldview, I headed off to college at the University of California in Berkeley. The Berkeley students seemed to be the vanguard of a vibrant spiritual awakening that followed the famous 1967 Summer of Love. Within a month, I had been initiated into transcendental meditation after seeing Maharishi Mahesh Yogi. I started to attend different spiritual gatherings, practically every night of the week. How I squeezed in my academic study is still a mystery to me.

One of my favorite gathering spots in Berkeley was the Blue Mountain Center of Meditation, located only a block from my cottage. There I learned more about integrating meditation into a daily life dedicated to spiritual learning. Sri Eknath Easwaran is still one of my spiritual heroes. I also had the good fortune to learn from my best friend, Bob, of the spiritual master Avatar Meher Baba, who was still living in India at that time.

Meher Baba's teachings, recorded in *The Discourses* and *God Speaks,* clarified and amplified the esoteric teachings I had learned in theosophy. And he added the missing ingredient to my spiritual quest: the love for God.

In 1952, Meher Baba organized a small group of American Sufis and wrote its charter. This group, Sufism Reoriented, was centered in San Francisco. I recognized the murshida, Ivy Duce, as the teacher I had been seeking. Thus, in 1970, I was initiated as a Sufi student under Baba's guidance.

What are my credentials for writing a book about the hidden spiritual energies underlying life processes? I have no spiritual authority whatsoever. I'm not a guru, a spiritual teacher, or even a counselor. I am, however, a seeker on the spiritual path, with many years of experience behind me. Though I'm not psychic, these years of study and meditation have opened up a certain intuitive perception within me that allows me to sense how occult processes work in the world.

This book, however, will definitely not give spiritual advice to fellow students. I offer no advice. In these pages, I will share my own insights, observations, and experiences, and my hope is that this will result in a fascinating and helpful collection of essays. Each chapter is an independent discussion about a particular aspect of life. Since the ideas are my personal opinions and insights, the reader is, of course, free to take or leave them. I offer these ideas for your consideration, not to accept as some lofty truth.

My Sufi training over these past years has formed the foundation for this book. My Sufi teachers are proponents of descendant spirituality. According to our principles, this is the spiritual impulse for this new age. In the past, the spiritual path has been defined as ascendant spirituality. This means that the seeker ascends out of the clutches of maya, materialistic illusion, to experience lighter, brighter, and more vibrant realms of spiritual reality. In the past, yogis have gained spiritual consciousness by meditation in secluded ashrams, far removed from the everyday world. Christian seekers have likewise sought out nunneries and monasteries to provide the best setting for the spiritual life. And it worked. This was a helpful and enlightening way of life that assisted seekers in past epochs.

Descendant spirituality works differently. Living spiritual principles in everyday life in the world is now the high road to divine vision. God is everywhere and is in everything. Likewise, the spiritual path is now everywhere and in everything. Sri Aurobindo is one spokesman for this new impulse. He said, "In the past spiritual development has been attempted by drawing away from the world and a disappearance into the Self or Spirit." Speaking of himself in the third person, Sri Aurobindo further states, "Sri Aurobindo teaches that a descent of the higher principle is possible which will not merely release the spiritual Self out of the world, but release it in the world, replace the mind's ignorance or its very limited knowledge, by a supramental Truth-consciousness which will be a sufficient instrument of the inner self and make it possible for the human being to find himself dynamically, as well as inwardly, and grow out of his still animal nature into a divine race" (Sri Aurobindo, *On Himself*, 1972).

If human beings are to manifest divine force and divine love in everyday life, it seems to me it's important to study the hidden side of life. It's interesting to learn how unseen energies interface with us constantly. An Egyptian architect, Dr. Ibrahim Karim, introduces the subject of my book masterfully on his website: "We are all dynamic living energy systems, existing in a sea of energy vibrations that is our world. Our vital energy systems are in constant interaction with each other and with our environment, exchanging energy effects on all levels" (www. Biogeometry.com).

Sri Aurobindo also seems to encourage the theme of this book: "Spiritual knowledge without the occult science lacks in precision and certainty in its objective effects; it is all-powerful only in the subjective world. The two, when combined, whether for external or internal actions, are irresistible and become an instrument fit for the manifestation of the Supramental Power" (Sri Aurobindo, *A Practical Guide to Integral Yoga*, 1971, p 280).

With these few introductory remarks, we're ready to begin. First, however, we need to clarify some metaphysical assumptions that underlie our discussions and also develop a precise vocabulary.

CHAPTER 1

Some Background

In my first book, *The Secret Life of Kids*, I discussed the existence and functions of the mind in the various subtle membranes of consciousness in order to explain how child development works from the spiritual perspective and show how children can be sensitive to the psychic realms. In dealing with the current topic of how subtle energy works on earth and affects us in our daily lives, such a metaphysical background is even more critical.

Obviously, the first assumption necessary to understanding subtle energies is that this outside world or environment we perceive with our normal senses is merely the outer crust of a vibratory reality that contains worlds within worlds of objective existence that are physically imperceptible.

Our inner being and the inner essence of all objects and living things in the world exist in different stages of expression and manifestation, corresponding to different dimensions or levels of more subtle, objective existence.

In the same way as the physical body simultaneously exists as atoms, as chemical combinations, as organs, each level with its corresponding environment, other aspects of our inner being are constructed of different degrees of refined matter and exist in corresponding subtle environments, each of which interpenetrates the physical world.

In this book, I'm going to use certain terms and make certain assumptions that come from the core of my own personal beliefs of how the world works and why it works the way it does. Although it may seem like a digression to sketch out a personal philosophy of life at this point, to me it is essential.

My views have evolved over fifty years of study and experience. My concepts of life started to coalesce during my teen years as a student in the Theosophical Society. These ideas were enhanced and clarified when I joined Meher Baba's Sufism Reoriented group.

Let me start with a metaphysical description of a human being. The divine essence of all—the core of a human being—is referred to variously as "atma," "monad," "soul," or "spirit." This atma projects itself into realms of manifested, objective reality in stages, wrapping around itself increasingly complex and solid sheaths of consciousness, or levels of being. These levels assist in the process of developing and expressing myriad aspects of the unfolding consciousness of the atma. At the same time, each succeeding sheath, more dense than the previous one, inevitably dulls and deadens the person to the simple, free-flowing levels of life energy represented by the subtler planes. In a general way, the more subtle of these inner energies connect us to aspects of being that exist beyond normal waking consciousness. Everyday awareness of subjective and emotional states works through denser and more material sheaths.

Flowing energies in the outside world can be registered in our waking awareness because people have the same corresponding levels of energy in their various membranes of consciousness. It's really the dense physical body that is mostly responsible for blocking the awareness of subtler life forces.

It's important to develop a vocabulary in referring to energies of consciousness, so that we may differentiate the levels of objective forces in the world that affect these inner membranes and therefore register within us as thoughts, feelings, or sensations.

The first, most refined vehicle of manifested life expression is often called the "causal body," though the word "body" seems inappropriate, as this sheath has little form or substance from a concrete perspective. It is created out of coded units of mind, called in Sanskrit *sanskaras*. Sanskaras represent the residue of all our life experiences from this and previous incarnations. In this higher level of mind (sometimes called buddhi-manas), these sanskaras are in a nonactivated, latent state. This aspect of being creates the causes of future mental expression, hence the term "causal body."

This sheath of consciousness, from the ordinary psychological perspective, could be described as the deepest layer of the unconscious mind. A person is aware of sanskaras only when they erupt into conscious expression. This highest mental aspect, then, does not represent the mind of concrete or even abstract thinking that we ordinarily experience, but it can be said to be the root source or cause of the mind.

Human consciousness is further expressed through what is termed the lower mind (in Sanskrit, *kama manas*). Meher Baba refers to this membrane as the subtle body. This level of mind is impregnated with desires and intimately bound to earthly life. Previously unmanifested sanskaras gain energy at this level and project into partial manifestation, gaining a fuller range of expression. But rather than considering this denser material to be matter, it is more helpful to consider the subtle level of mind simply as energy. Thus, the pure mind of the causal body consolidates into the energy of the subtle body or kama manas, where it is partially expressed.

The "mind" referred to here is not the intellectual functions commonly associated with the word, but rather the essence of conscious life. The Buddha remarked that man is nothing but mind. From this perspective, the denser, lower sheaths are simply different expressions of mind. At the level of the subtle body, this mind-plus-energy expresses itself as concrete thoughts combined with emotion. Since thoughts and emotions are not really separate from one another, the thinking aspect of the mind is reflected energetically and concretely, along with desires and emotions, in this layer of consciousness.

Meher Baba summed up manifested creation by stating that matter is consolidated energy, while energy is consolidated mind. If one referred to the causal body as the "unconscious mind," then one could refer to the subtle body as the "subconscious mind."

The lower three membranes, which are constructed of subtle mind-energy now solidified as particles of matter (physical and super-physical), represent the expression of essential mind as a manifested personality in incarnation on earth. Therefore, while the higher sheaths have a certain permanent existence, the lower three vehicles come and go as birth and death connect them to or disconnect them from earthly fields of expression. These three layers in cosmos, earth, and human represent the occult foundations for the discussions in this book.

These three lower sheaths are generally called the "astral body," the "etheric body," and the "physical body." These three work in close harmony, expressing mental and emotional impulses in external activity in the physical world. They also, as will be shown in the chapter on medicine, work together to sustain physical life processes.

According to Dr. Rudolf Steiner, a spiritual teacher active in Europe during the early decades of the twentieth century, the animal kingdom also shares with human beings the etheric and astral counterparts to the physical vehicle. The plant kingdom only shares the etheric connection.

Even though the astral and etheric bodies are closely bound up with physical processes, particularly in the endocrine, circulatory, and nervous systems, people are usually only indirectly aware of the astral and etheric aspects of such mechanisms. In a sense, our awareness of these levels of life is mostly subjective, unrelated to concrete, sensory experiences. My teacher, Dr. James MacKie, successor to Murshida Ivy Duce of Sufism Reoriented, would sometimes refer to the astral body as the personality or ego in incarnation.

In this book, I'm asking the reader to conceptually bridge the gap between subjective feelings and thoughts and objective, sensory perceptions in realms of everyday life. Becoming sensitive to the flow of etheric currents in life, lying just beyond or behind physical processes, is a delightful way to fill life with excitement and meaning. It's descendant spirituality at its most concrete level. As the theosophical leader Madame H. P. Blavatsky once said, "Occult forces, beneficent and maleficent, ever [surround] us and manifest their presence in various ways." Studying these forces is the theme of this book.

I like to use the term "etheric currents" to refer to the life force here on earth. The Chinese use the word *chi* to describe this energy. In Sanskrit, it's often called *prana*. The drawback to the term prana is that there is pranic life force on all planes of existence; physical prana is only the most dense form. Etheric force, however, only refers to that membrane of life just behind physical objectivity. The term "vital force" or "vital body" has also been used to denote the energies discussed in this book. Spiritual writers from Sri Aurobindo to the astrologer Max Heindel use the term "vital force." In these expositions, however, I will largely stick to the term "etheric force."

As the mind manifests coded sanskaric light fibers from the causal body, these sanskaras attract matter from denser levels, which encrust the sanskaras and allow for manifested expression. Murshid MacKie once told me that the etheric body is composed of the "roots" of physical sanskaric fibers that build the tissue of the outer body. In fact, new sanskaras are created by every thought, word, or deed expressed in incarnate life. The etheric body, then, is the mold of mental conditioning (sanskaras) creating the body and its subjective life.

Meher Baba in his writings explains basic life patterns in terms of sanskaras. Partially expressed sanskaras in the subtle body create the conditioned impulses from past lives that manifest the astral, etheric, and physical vehicles. Residual sanskaras from the past manifest genetic tendencies, from eye color to temperament. Then, as a lifetime continues, we express and create sanskaras through all activities. Life is nothing but the conditioned mind expressing itself and then gathering more and more conditioning.

Meher Baba called this process "winding" sanskaras. Ultimately, in spiritual lives, the goal is to spend the old sanskaras, while not allowing newly created ones to stick; hence the importance put on detachment in most spiritual systems.

Sanskaras from myriad past lifetimes have been wound on the core of the mind in the causal body. This core is sometimes referred to as the heart. Spiritual experiences in light-filled inner realms are unveiled as the mass of sanskaras are thinned out, unwound, or burned away.

I am emphasizing this concept of sanskaras, of course, first because I have found the concept so helpful in understanding life processes, from sleeping and waking to talents and careers, to friends and mates, to life and death. Also, sanskaras are coded subtle units of energy. And this book is about energies of life found everywhere. Therefore, I find the idea of sanskaras foundational.

Everything around us has sanskaras. Animals and plants embody their own sanskaras. Inanimate things like furniture and machines collect the sanskaras of their owners. Houses, public buildings, or mass transit all hold sanskaras of the people who have used them. I remember my first spiritual teacher, Murshida Duce, used to tell her students when we were out in public, putting our hands on railings or doors, to always shake our hands to eliminate sanskaras we might have picked up from other people. Of course, the common habit of washing hands after being in public places accomplishes the same thing.

To more fully understand sanskaras, an anecdote from Meher Baba's sister might be helpful. Meher Baba first published his book, *God Speaks*, in 1955. American disciples were trying to understand Baba's concepts and sent questions to Mani, Baba's sister. One question was about sanskaras. Mani wrote to an American devotee, "In my words and interpretation, it comes to this: while we are in one body, we gather the sanskaras for the next one, preparing the skeleton, as it were, choosing, selecting and fixing the material. The body is an illusion because it is nothing but a pack of sanskaras. It is absolutely nothing but sanskaras piled up on top of each other. When the sanskaras are used up, the body naturally drops. There is nothing else to be done, as body and sanskaras are one and the same thing—no sanskaras, no physical body" *(A Love So Amazing,* p 90).

Much more will be said about these sanskaric threads of life, as we continue our journey to observe how subtle energies affect all of us every day, in little and not-so-little ways in our daily lives.

CHAPTER 2

Water

The twentieth-century sage from South India, Ramana Maharshi, once said, "What is in the world is in the [human] body, and what is in the body is in the world also." In these pages, many energy connections are examined that link our Mother Earth to our own being. One of these connections has to do with water. The earth is approximately 70 percent water, and the human body is approximately 65 percent water. Water is a huge part of our outer environment, as it is a huge part of our inner environment.

Life originally came from the waters of the earth, and water continues to sustain life. Everyone knows that many physicians recommend people drink eight glasses of water each day. And when recovering from illness, most doctors say, "Drink plenty of water." But from the occult point of view, water is more than a healing drink. Indeed, it is almost more miraculous than you can believe.

From the perspective of Chinese geomancy, a mountain peak would embody positive or masculine energy, and a lake in a valley would represent negative or feminine energy. Water is receptive. From an energy point of view, water accepts a charge and can be energized from many different realms. Water can be electrified with prana, or as the nineteenth-century occultists used to say, water can be magnetized, that is, become surcharged with etheric force.

A personal hero of mine who was on the leading edge of research into how the subjective, inner worlds impact the objective, outer world is the late, great Japanese scientist, Dr. Masaru Emoto. I was fortunate to personally meet Dr. Emoto at a lecture in 2010 at the New Living Expo in San Francisco. The interesting thing about his presentation is it was all in Japanese; he spoke no English. So his comments on water and climate change all had to be translated as he spoke. In his research he has shown definitively how the etheric energies of the earth and of man can affect water, alter water, and enliven water. To me, this research is so mind-boggling, that if every human being examined and understood Dr. Emoto's data, not a single concept outlined in this book would seem the least bit far-fetched.

To introduce Dr. Emoto's work, let me quote from the preface to his book, *The Hidden Messages of Water*:

> Using high speed photography, Dr. Masaru Emoto discovered that crystals found in frozen water reveal change when specific, concentrated thoughts are directed toward them. He found that water from clear springs and water that has been exposed to loving words show brilliant, complex, and colorful snowflake patterns. In contrast, polluted water, or water exposed to negative thoughts forms incomplete, asymmetrical patterns with dull colors. The implications of this research create a new awareness of how we can positively impact the earth and our personal health.

I will summarize some of his experiments. He would start with two glasses of filtered water. Dr. Emoto found that the chlorine and fluoride in unfiltered, processed water did not produce clear crystals when quickly frozen. That fact in and of itself demonstrates the importance of filtering our processed water in order to maximize its nutritional and energy benefits. Anyhow, these two glasses of water would be treated by the spoken word. Dr. Emoto would say, "I love you," to one glass and say, "I hate you," to the other glass. When a sample of each glass of water was quickly frozen, the love glass formed magnificent, balanced crystals, whereas the hate glass formed twisted, lopsided, blunt crystals. The conclusion: Human speech connected with concentrated thoughts has an altering effect on dense matter, in this case the very structure of water.

Dr. Emoto repeated the experiments by only exposing the glasses of water to the thought *I love you* or *I hate you*; there were no words spoken. When quickly frozen, the crystal formations were identical. He then wrote the words "love" and "hate" and taped them on the glasses of water for some time. The effect with the water crystals was the same.

These clear, beautiful, sometimes colorful crystals were created with variations, when exposed to any positive or happy thought; words like "health," "peace," or "happiness" all had powerful effects on the crystals. Exposure to music also had effects. Heavy-metal music played to a glass of water created asymmetrical crystals, whereas Bach or Mozart gave rise to lovely, snowflake forms.

At New Age shops these days, you can buy little stickers that say "love" or "peace" to put on glasses of water to positively charge water at your own home. When I first found out about Dr. Emoto's work, I would take a glass of filtered water at my school and have four or five children whisper into the glass, "I love you" or "Thank you." It was fun imagining how the structure of water was being altered. And the children loved the process too. They thought it was very cute to say, "I love you," to a glass of water.

The structure of the cells of water was being altered. Wow. Let's look at this statement. The ancient sage Zoroaster said that the foundation for a spiritual life is "good thoughts, good words, and good deeds." Now Dr. Emoto discovers that good thoughts, good words, and good deeds alter the actual forms of material substances. In another interesting example, Dr. Emoto had a group of one hundred Zen Buddhist monks chant by the side of a very polluted lake in Japan. After an hour of chanting, the water crystals changed from lopsided and distorted to beautiful and symmetrical. Thoughts are things, and words carry etheric and astral energies out into the world. They can literally affect and change the outer world. In former times, occultists who wanted to change the outer world through thoughts, words, and ceremonial deeds were called magicians. Dr. Emoto proved that, knowingly or unknowingly, all of us are magicians.

At my home, I have a special glass I keep on the kitchen windowsill. I energize the filtered water in the glass in many ways. Of course, I talk to the water, usually saying, "I love you," or "Thank you," before I drink it. I also expose the water to direct sunlight. I have heard that sunlight can surcharge a glass of water. Further, the glass sits on a little magnet pad I purchased from the Edgar Cayce group. Apparently exposing water to magnets aligns the molecules in some way, which makes the water easier to absorb. I also obtained a swizzle stick made of the gemstone tourmaline, which has been shown to alkalize water. My diet, although filled with plenty of fruits and vegetables, is still too acidic. Sometimes, I pour my glass of water three times over a necklace of aquamarine beads.

Michael Katz, who founded the group specializing in the therapeutic effects of wearing gemstone necklaces, also developed the concept behind what he calls aquamarine water. Aquamarine crystals radiate healing energy (see my chapter on the mineral kingdom). Here's Michael Katz:

> As its name implies, aquamarine has a special relationship with water. Aquamarine energy resonates with the fluidity of this primal element, both on our planet and with our bodies.
>
> In part because of this resonance, water can easily be infused with the energy of aquamarine. Drinking the resulting Aquamarine Water brings this vitalizing energy directly to the body's cells. (Michael Katz, *Aquamarine Water, Fountain of Youthful Vitality*)

Drinking water that's been treated in all these ways (which are so simple to put into practice) hasn't reversed the effects of aging or given me infinite vitality. But I do feel confident that drinking water helps us in many ways, and using esoteric knowledge to energize water certainly can't hurt us. And, I'll admit, it's fun to use occult forces to help heal and vitalize my physical body.

Treated water can also be used in the garden, healing and helping the earth. In the early 1920s, Dr. Steiner started the biodynamic gardening impulse. He recommended several techniques to surcharge water with energies of growth and fertility, and suggested to use this super water in the garden. One specific preparation particularly appeals to me because it's based on utilizing unseen forces of the earth. To make this preparation, you take fresh cow manure, preferably from cows near the garden property, and pack the manure into a cow's horn. Then you bury the horn in the earth during late fall and allow it to remain in the ground during the winter months. In the spring, you dig up the cow horn, put small portions of the packed manure into water, and sprinkle this in the garden.

What's the purpose of this odd gardening practice? This is the explanation as I understand it, as I'm not really an experienced student of biodynamic agriculture: The function of the horn of a cow, when it's connected to the cow, is to focus concentrated etheric energy from the surrounding atmosphere into the cow's body to help it with the difficult task of digesting grass. The horn works like a pyramidal form to collect and focus energy. When the cow horn is packed with manure, the horn's function continues, and the manure becomes super manure due to the force irradiating it. When this irradiation process happens within Mother Earth, it's the earth energies of growth that surcharge the manure. In the astrology chapter, I discuss how the earth energies are fully breathed into the earth during the winter months. Thus, life on top of the earth seems dead, while life forces are breathed into the earth, where they wait for spring in latent, potential form.

Dr. Steiner suggested a gardener might take advantage of these earth forces during the winter months by burying the manure-horn preparation in the earth. In the spring, the cow horn is unburied. Small amounts of the manure preparation mixed in water can make the water into sort of a super fertilizing substance—let's say kind of a plant super vitamin.

There are other ways to charge water in biodynamic agriculture. One that I recall involves soaking stinging nettle plants in water for a week and then sprinkling that nettle-charged water in the garden. When I garden, I sometimes use my own vital force to charge watering cans. I'll dip the ends of my fingers of my right hand into the water in the watering can and say out loud, "Water, be thou blessed." I can feel myself tapping into feelings from a past life as a Catholic priest. But why not take advantage of that sense that we humans can channel the power of God and use it to bless?

That brings me to the subject of using blessed water, holy water, in the Roman Catholic liturgy. Catholic priests have known for centuries that water has a receptive nature and can hold a blessing or a charge. It can be electrified and used for helpful purposes. In the Liberal Catholic Church, founded by C. W. Leadbeater, this is the procedure for the priest to sanctify water. The priest says the following words:

> Oh, God, who for the helping and safeguarding of man
> dost hallow the water set apart for the service of thy holy
> church, send forth thy light and thy power upon this
> element of water which we bless and hallow in thy holy
> name. Grant that whoever uses this water in faithfulness
> of spirit may be strengthened in all goodness and that
> everything sprinkled with it may be made holy and pure
> and guarded from all assaults of evil, through Christ our
> Lord, amen. (*The Liturgy*, 1967, p 398)

There is no doubt of the power that this blessed water holds. My wife and I recently visited a newly built cathedral in Oakland, California. As we sat quietly, I mentioned to Hana that spiritual force (called *baraka* in Sufism) sure takes a long time to build up in a church. This new church seemed empty of the kind of energies you feel in cathedrals in Europe that have been used for Christian worship for hundreds of years. As we were leaving the sanctuary, Hana called over to me and said, "Here's the church's baraka, Jim." She was standing by an unusually large font of holy water. I joined her. The spiritual force radiating from the water was palpable.

Psychic healers often use charged water for curing various ailments. The first president of the Theosophical Society, Colonel Henry Olcott, would examine a patient and then take a pure silver straw and blow on a glass of water, with the intent of healing the particular condition of his patient. He would instruct the patient to take sips of the water at various times of the day. Col. Olcott, by the way, had to stop using this healing technique because he was depleting his own reserve of etheric force by using it to heal others. Healers often make themselves ill by transferring their own life-giving prana energies to clients.

Dr. Steiner, the spiritual teacher who demonstrated in so many ways and in so many professional fields how to utilize occult energies in practical situations, described many ways to use water in healing. I have been interested in his anthroposophical medicine for decades and have taken several medical workshops. The anthroposophical nutritional bath is an example of the type of water treatments Dr. Steiner recommended.

You fill a bathtub with hot water and add three ingredients to the water: a raw egg, a small amount of milk, and a little honey. When the tub is full, you take the right hand and dip your fingertips in the water—maybe two inches—and trace a figure 8 (a lemniscate) in the water, following this pattern for a minute or two. Then you soak in this energized water. The three substances, milk, egg, and honey, have etheric energies that are transferred to the water. The egg in particular has tremendous etheric force. When you transfer your own forces to the water by touching the liquid in a moving figure 8, the healing effects of the water are completed.

I prepare a nutritional bath for myself whenever I feel I'm coming down with some twinge of an illness. The bath can help ward off a cold or flu. It's a good step to take in managing your own health. Of course, preparing a bath like this is a wonderful way to care for children or another family member. Knowing ways to use occult forces in practical matters adds an empowering and fun dimension to life.

Healing waters often come right out of the earth itself and need no treatment by human beings. All are familiar with the existence of healing wells, springs, and rivers in many parts of the world. Mineral baths, sulphur baths, and hot springs are quite common in volcanic areas. There are other springs where legends are told of physical healing taking place if you soak in the water or drink it. My only experience is with the healing water of the Chalice Well in Glastonbury, England. Here, it is said, Jesus's uncle, Joseph of Arimathea, hid the Holy Grail on one of his trading expeditions to England after the crucifixion of Jesus. Ever since then, legend has it, the well waters have flowed red as blood.

For centuries, hundreds of Europeans have visited Glastonbury to drink from this holy well. I can't claim to have been healed by the well water, but I did take a vial home to keep in my meditation room. I have the four elements in my meditation room: air, earth, fire, and water. And the vial of holy water comes from the Chalice Well.

I also remember drinking from the holy spring located at Mother Mary's house near Ephesus, Turkey. The fact that water can hold an energy charge makes it clear how some water can have healing power.

And then there is the Ganges River. In India, the mighty Ganges River, which begins in the Himalayas near the sacred town of Badrinath and empties into the Bay of Bengal, is considered sacred. A bath in the

Ganges is believed by Hindus to be a purifying experience. Sins are wiped away and swept down the river. And to die near the Ganges, or to have the ashes of one's dead body deposited in the Ganges, helps the soul in the next world and in some cases can even bestow salvation or nirvana on an individual.

In 1975, I bathed in the Ganges in Rishikesh, near where the Ganges rushes out of the mountains. Its water was milky white because it is mixed with crushed particles of rock from the high mountains. As with the Chalice Well, I didn't experience being purified of sin or even bad habits. But that could have been my fault. Many spiritual teachers discuss how your thoughts and beliefs affect your life. Strong thoughts manifest into reality. If you bathe in the Ganges and strongly believe you will be purified, then I'm sure the results can be efficacious. In any event, it's just one more example of the power, the energy, and the miracle of water.

CHAPTER 3

Astrology

As with so many aspects of the hidden side of life, I discovered the efficacy and practicality of astrology through the normal course of events. As a happy and successful schoolteacher for forty-two years, I always noticed one thing: My mood and efficiency in dealing with thirty children seemed to change daily. I could never be satisfied or rest on my accomplishments, because every day seemed so unique. Early in my teaching career, I noticed there would be certain days when I felt spaced out, scattered, disorganized, and impatient with the children. This quality of consciousness did not seem to correlate with how well prepared my lessons were, my health, or how I slept the previous night. This scattered feeling just was there, and it lasted throughout the day. I don't remember if a friend suggested it, or if I thought of it myself, but one day, I started analyzing what zodiacal sign the moon was in during one of my difficult days. It was always in one of the air signs: Libra, Aquarius, or Gemini.

This designation of air sign has to do with the four medieval elements: air, earth, fire, and water. The concept of four elements that form our outside world is familiar and useful to spiritual students, but not generally accepted by materialistic people. Anyhow, in astrology, there are three signs in each element.

The moon represents the personality. As the moon moves through the celestial heavens, the tone or vibrancy changes according to which sign it is in. I noticed that every time I had an extremely oppositional day, the moon was always in an air sign. I would have one of those days, check my astrological calendar, discover that, yup, the moon was in an air sign, and then give myself a pass for the day. "I'm not a bad teacher, after all. The moon was just in an air sign."

I am a Pisces, which is a water sign. As I looked at it, the air of the moon, interacting with the water of my sun sign, created waves. After a while, I began to check before a new day began. If the moon was in an air sign, I would gird my loins, take a deep breath, and decide this day was going to work out just fine. If I started getting unusually impatient with the kids, I would stop, reset myself, and think, *That's just the difficult lunar energy interacting with my energy field.*

So I learned early in my adult life that astrology is not just a silly superstition. As a footnote to this discussion, as I finished writing these few introductory paragraphs, I wandered through my house, trying to decide what to work on next. I got a familiar spaced-out feeling and scattered attention. I went over to my astrological calendar, and guess what? The moon was in Libra. On the other side of the coin, I have also noticed that when I need to give a lecture or presentation, it is often very helpful if the moon is in an air sign. Air stimulates intellect, and articulating ideas in a lecture can be thus amplified. It's also a good time to fly in an airplane.

When human beings take a new incarnation on this earth, they have to balance their connections to all the energies of the earth, the sun, the moon, and the cosmos. The study of these energies and how they affect humans as they reincarnate is called astrology. No treatise on how hidden energies affect us could be complete without considering astrology.

Some astrologers say that no one really knows how astrology works in the energy structure of a human being. But they are certain that it does.

The late, great founder of the Philosophical Research Society, Manly Palmer Hall, wrote a magnificent little book in 1943, called *The Philosophy of Astrology.* In this book, he offers the only explanation I have found as to how astrological configurations actually affect our energy fields:

> We see that the life which flows from the stars is gathered
> up and reflected through the temperaments of the planets
> and radiated into the etheric field of the Earth. From the
> Earth it is redistributed into the organism of all organic
> creatures to become the vitality of those creatures and
> the sustaining power of their various functions. Each

order evolving in nature manifests this vitality through an evolutionary process. Growth is the release of cosmic energy through form. The energies first build and perfect suitable organisms and flow through these organisms as function. (*The Philosophy of Astrology*, 1976, p 61)

So when a baby is born and takes that first breath in the outside world, after being in the protective womb of its mother, something miraculous occurs. The blends of energy in the cosmos, at that exact moment of this first breath, penetrate (even condition, you might say) the very cells of the body. At that precise moment, the exact blend of forces, the currents of life from the sun, moon, earth, and planets, creates a sort of force field around the baby's body. My late Murshid called this energetic web the "astrological sheath." This sheath exists between the membranes I'm calling the subtle and the astral bodies. The shape of this living web is different for each astrological sign. And it lives and grows in tandem with the gross, physical body throughout a lifetime, obviously having its effects on the living personality. All sanskaric forces from the higher planes filter through the astrological sheath and are modified by the time they reach the physical brain. This sheath defines how life energies will integrate with the astral body, the personality, in incarnation.

I remember Murshid describing the sheath of a Leo. He said it looked like a dancer with a big hoop skirt or a dervish whirling with the ends of his robe connecting to the earth and an opening in the middle, allowing forces from the sun to shine through. He said a Leo loves to just sit in the middle of a circle of friends, the hoops of his skirt vibrating up and down, and holding forth like a great and luminous king. I can remember a few other configurations of astrological sheaths. Aries, for example, is a column of energy going straight up. Gemini looks like a bundle of wires sticking out every which way. The sheath of a Libra actually has the structure of a balance scale, and Murshid commented that when the scales of Libras were in perfect balance, they could guide others with tremendous authority.

The astrological sheath, however, is not a true mechanism of consciousness. It's more like a filter or a lens on a camera. If the mental and subtle bodies represent the actual working parts of the camera, and the photos produced represent experiences in the physical body, the astrological sheath would be a tint or a filter on the camera. All the sanskaric impressions take on this particular tint as they pass into physical expression. The tint or filter of Cancers makes all their experiences different from those of an Aquarian.

Let me give you a true-life example from a few days ago. My wife and I were on a retirement trip to Hawaii and the island of Maui. We took a two-day excursion to the beautiful, tropical side of the island called the "Road to Hana" (Hana is the town at the end of the road).

Anyway, Hana and I were studying the twenty pages of our Maui guidebook dedicated to the wonderful sights of this tropical road. I, being a Pisces, focused on which tropical waterfalls we should stop at and where would be a good spot for lunch. Hana, being a Taurus, zeroed in on the one or two sentences that warned that sometimes thieves would see something in your car while you were hiking to a waterfall, break in, and steal it. So she spent some time strategizing with me about what we could leave in the back seat of the car and what we should lock up in the trunk. Her Taurus filter, which is prone to pay attention to security concerns, latched onto an issue that my little Piscean brain filter was completely oblivious to.

Another interesting aspect of astrology is that so much is based on the forces and aspects of the sun. Mexican philosophers call the sun the "right eye of God." My teacher used to say God was "the sun behind the sun behind the sun." The theosophists referred to God energy as the "solar Logos" or the "word" of the sun. (Madame Blavatsky was asked if there was God. She replied, "Let's just say that the sun is the ambassador of the deity" [*The Secret Doctrine Commentaries*, 2010].) If this sun supports life on the earth, why wouldn't the tremendous bursts of light and force of our sun also affect our personalities?

In Rudolf Steiner's Waldorf schools, children in the early grades are encouraged to venerate the forces of the sun and earth. One poem for first-graders goes like this:

> The golden sun so great and bright
> Warms the world with all its might.
> It makes the dark earth green and fair,
> Attends each thing with ceaseless care.
> It shines on blossom, stone, and tree,

On bird and beast, on you and me.
Oh may each deed throughout the day,
May everything we do and say,
Be bright and strong and true
O golden sun like you.

But what about all the astrological lingo about the moon and the planets in this or that sign? Critics who debunk astrology say, "What possible effect could the distant light of Neptune, say, have on human temperaments? Even the sun and the moon; okay, the light of the sun helps plants grow, and the phases of the moon affect ocean tides. But saying I feel and act a certain way because my sun is in Pisces and my moon is in Cancer? Give me a break. It's all nonsense."

In fact, just yesterday, my scientist brother emailed me and said exactly that. And he further said, "How could you include a chapter in your book on this silly topic, astrology? Who will ever read the book when you write such bunk?" My brother, of course, says the same thing when I use homeopathic medicine: "That is all nonsense; how could homeopathy have any scientific validity?"

The scientific paradigm of the Newtonian age needs to shift to understand any concept in this book. Fortunately, quantum physics is spearheading that shift. I will further discuss homeopathic medicine in my chapter on medicine.

Light coming from the planets seems minuscule, but that does not mean that that light is not connected to flowing energy. Let's take Mars energy as an example. The sight of the reddish light you can see coming from Mars on a clear night confirms that there certainly is Mars energy of some sort reaching the earth. Of course, light from the planets is still reflected solar light, as is the moon's light. Since light is the physical manifestation of subtle energy, one can understand the sun's subtle energy bounces off planets and, as Manly Hall stated, that reflected energy takes on the temperament of each planet. Obviously, we're speaking mostly of energy from the invisible realms, the etheric and astral planes.

The sun, moon, and planets represent the energy that provides the basis for astrological charts, or the pictures of where the cosmic energies were positioned relative to the earth at the time of your birth. The fixed stars in the constellations have little to do with it. To say your Venus is in Scorpio means that when you were born, the Venus energy was streaming down on the earth at a specific angle. It's the angle of energy that counts. Think of the angle of the sun's energy. At sunrise, the angle of solar light often creates beautiful colors. In the early morning, the sun's light could be shining in your eyes. At noon, the sun's energies are beating down on your head and making you hot. So the angle of light or energy makes a difference.

But what if the moon was on the opposite side of the earth when you were born? How could lunar energies affect you? One teacher I heard referred to the "transparent earth." The physical earth does not impede these cosmic energies we are discussing. Astral forces are made of much finer particles than the densest physical matter, so astral particles can pass through dense matter. If lunar energies can pass through this transparent earth to help build your astrological sheath, perhaps such energies are amplified after passing through the earth.

As early as 1889, Madame H. P. Blavatsky spoke about "planetary spirits" in her book *The Secret Doctrine*. And in 2010, the author of *Subtle Worlds*, David Spangler, discussed planetary spirits and even "trans-planetary spirit." Most probably, these cosmic intelligences also have to do with the radiating energies of the planets and their effects on astrological charts. However, I do not know enough about this topic to discuss it intelligently. As a wise old Sufi once said to me, "It probably has something to do with something."

Of course, all this is, as Maimonides would say, my own opinion. I have studied the effects of astrology for fifty years and speculated on how it works. The next part of this discussion has to do with the practical side of understanding the existence and effects of the astrological energies on your everyday life.

Certain aspects of life and personality can become forceful and dynamic as the moon waxes towards the full. And any teacher, like myself, can confirm that during a full moon, the classroom is often energetic and challenging. I actually discussed with my children the word "lunatic" coming from "luna," or moon. I would say, "Today's the full moon, so try not to be a lunatic (or sometimes I say "moonatic"). If you feel like hitting someone or putting them down, just think, *This full moon is pushing me into breaking school rules, and I don't have to be bullied by the moon.*

Also, scheduling more active games or hikes on full moon days is helpful. A soccer game would be a better full moon sport than a sitting game like "duck, duck goose." You can help kids to use and channel their excess energies.

But what is the occult side of this energized full moon? I must again refer to a casual comment from my Murshid MacKie, which clarified so much for me. He said that the moon is a dead earth of an ancient epoch of the past, and now the moon is disintegrating in a sort of "radioactive" way. It's always radiating subtle particles of matter. During the full moon, more of these particles are bombarding us than at any other time of the month. As the subtle hailstones hit your aura, they can either energize you, or they can be a very agitating influence in your life (or both).

The other side of the month, the dark of the moon, the new moon, can also be an energetic day. Starting projects or jobs or new phases of life with the new moon and allowing the natural forces of the cosmos to assist in your endeavor can be a helpful practice. My first teacher, Murshida Duce, used to always start her White Pony School on the new moon. Even if the new moon did not correspond to the calendars of neighboring school districts, Murshida was firm on starting the new school year with the new moon.

Even as the moon has phases, there are other important junctures in the astronomical year that you can be aware of. The first is the change of sun signs. As I clarified, the sun really is the root of understanding all occult aspects behind astrology. As the sun passes through the signs of the zodiac, its vibratory pattern changes. Thus, a Pisces sun in the springtime would feel different than a Scorpio sun in the late fall. Being aware of these monthly cosmic transitions can make astrology an interesting addition to understanding the world around you.

Murshid MacKie was extremely sensitive to these transitions, and when the sun moved into a new sign, he often had to withdraw into seclusion for a few hours or even a day to equilibrate the new flow of energies into his etheric structure.

Four times a year, there are rather more dramatic transitions of natural forces that people in ancient times used to commemorate with grand festivals. These are the vernal and autumnal equinoxes and the summer and winter solstices.

Dr. Steiner explained the importance of these four momentous days in terms of the understanding of the living earth. The earth, he said, is a living organism, and the astrological year represents a complete breath of the earth. Starting at the summer solstice in June, the earth starts to breathe slowly in. Murshid MacKie called this event the "spiritual new year." The breath of the earth is fully expelled at the summer solstice, and the life on the surface of the earth is most active. The earth's breath is completely breathed in as winter solstice approaches. On December 21, the etheric earth starts to breathe out again. But even though the out-breath starts slowly, the earth is at its most inner, quiet phase, cold and lifeless, during the winter months.

One interesting aspect of this earth activity is to note that the earth is then carrying out the opposite activity in the Southern Hemisphere: the breathing is reversed. Earth starts the out-breath at the summer solstice and the in-breath at the winter solstice (with respect to the Northern Hemisphere).

I've been to many ancient temples, like New Grange in Ireland and Stonehenge in England, where these earth-energy commemorations were celebrated. Ancient peoples knew the importance of these astronomical transitions since they were more conscious than modern people of these energies radiating throughout the world at these times. And they honored them with ritual.

During my teaching career, it seemed important to have children celebrate the transition of the winter solstice. Children, in their development, recapitulate in consciousness the phases of historical development of humankind as a whole. This is known as "Ontogeny recapitulates phylogeny." I have found that children will very solemnly enjoy the solstice commemoration of the energies of the sun and earth.

Since the sun is farthest away from earth during this time, and life is, so to speak, diminished, we celebrate the symbolic bringing of more life and light to earth, as the earth starts slowly breathing out. In my classroom ritual, the children stand in a circle. On the floor of the classroom are pine boughs, marking a spiral path to the center altar. On this altar is the "sun," a candle situated in a nest of crystals. Each child walks individually on the path to the center of the circle, while I recite, "Peter is walking now to get his little light. All the stars are watching by the day and by the night." Peter now lights his individual candle from the light of the sun. "Now he has his little light, and his eyes are shining bright. Carefully he's bringing his light into the ring." When everyone has his or her light, we all sing this song:

> Down with darkness, up with light.
> Up with sunshine, down with night.
> Each of us is one small light,
> But together we shine bright.
> Go away darkness, blackest night.
> Go away, make way for light.

One can imagine what a powerful ritual this can be for seven-year-olds on a cold winter morning.

Speaking of children, I must end this chapter with a slightly different take on astrology. As any teacher can tell you, the energetic makeup of a new class in a new school year is utterly different from the class the year before, or the class the year before that. Each group of children offers a matrix of etheric energies that blend together, making the class a happy, easy group for the teacher, or a challenging, difficult group, or something in between. Whether teachers know it or not, they are practical believers in Chinese astrology.

Chinese astrology is based on the lunar year and is conceived by imagining that the lens of solar, cosmic, and planetary energies changes each year. The matrix of cosmic forces today is different than it was one year ago. According to legend, when Lord Buddha was on his deathbed, he summoned all the animals on earth to come and bid him goodbye. Only twelve beasts came. To reward these twelve, he told them that each would be in charge of one year in the twelve-year lunar cycle. Thus, one year is the year of the tiger, while another is the year of the ox, and so on. With this world view, people born during the lunar year of the monkey exhibit certain monkey-like characteristics. Similarly, children born during the year of the ox can be ox-like.

And an elementary school is a perfect laboratory for understanding the underlying principles of this brand of astrology. At no other time during your life are you so completely separated into groups according to the year you are born. Thus, one year a teacher's class will have a group of twenty-five fire snakes, whereas the next year, it'll be a class of earth oxen. How different their energies feel. I personally do not quite understand exactly how Chinese astrology works. I only know there certainly is truth to it.

Understanding astrology is one important key in comprehending how a host of vital, unseen forces mold the etheric body and thereby guide the aptitudes of the personality. A psychically sensitive woman I knew in the early 1970s used to refer to the etheric formative forces as "brain forces." Appreciating the structure of the etheric body and its brain force, built with astrological energies, helps us understand the inner secrets of life more fully.

CHAPTER 4

The Environment

This chapter is not about global warming, pollution, or recycling. It's not about climate change or about using alternative fuels to power our cars or heat our homes. It's about how the etheric forces of nature, the etheric forces of objects in our environment, and the accumulated etheric forces of the people around us affect our lives all the time and in every way.

It's very interesting to think of our environment as filled with colorful, living currents of swirling unseen energies. I spoke about the effects of the invisible electromagnetic radiations (EMRs) all around us in the chapter on technology. This chapter is about even subtler life forces that affect our thinking, moods, and emotions, and even our physical health, 24/7.

Let's begin with the subtle energies of the geographic area where you live. I cannot really discuss the energies of the entire world, but obviously the earth currents of the East are completely different from the energies of the West. It's no accident that the East has encouraged people to be more inner and spiritually oriented, and the West has supported people to seek more material prosperity and advancement in the outer world. The movement of personal energies in the human etheric field of people in the East tend to go "in and up," whereas in the West, this same human energy field encourages energies to go "down and out" and into the world.

Every country has its own energy grid. It is said, for instance, that the veil between the physical and etheric worlds is thinnest in Ireland. That is why more people are sensitive to the inner planes and see the fairy world there than in other countries.

California is similar to Ireland, but for a completely different reason. In California, we have more days of bright sunshine than in any other state of America. We absorb a type of pranic energy from the sun through the chakras in the abdomen. Charles Leadbeater, the theosophical seer, said that the sun's etheric field creates "vitality globules." You can sometimes see them on bright, sunny days. They are tiny sparks of light that twinkle just for a second and then are gone from sight. These vitality globules are absorbed by the chakras and circulate around your vital body by the etheric meridian grid spoken of in Chinese medicine. Because of the preponderance of absorbed solar energy, many people in California are psychically sensitive, and there are more spiritual groups and cults here than in other states. Again, as in Ireland, the veil between the astral realms and the gross sphere is thinner in California. These are powerful, multitasking currents that affect human life on every level.

I have many friends in Washington DC. One of the things they always mention when visiting California is how different the energy atmosphere is here. Some even have difficulty sleeping because the energy is wilder and more forceful.

Not only does the etheric earth energy of geographical locales affect our emotional and mental bodies but also the neighborhood we live in. Just meditate for a moment on the differences between living in the city versus living in the country. Most people who choose to live in the city say, "Oh, I want the cultural life of the city: the fine restaurants, the theaters, the museums." But I don't think that is all there is to it. Many people thrive on the stimulating etheric currents only found in the city.

As I discuss in the next chapter, the thoughts and feelings of human beings generate energy and crystalize into materialized forms on the astral plane. Those energetic forms are clearly much more numerous in the psychic atmosphere of the city. Indeed, they create the hum and buzz of city life.

I've always found it interesting to question travelers about their trips to foreign lands. "Where did you go in Europe?" I'll ask. "Oh, I went to London, Paris, and Rome," they reply. For many people, absorbing the sights, sounds, and thought forms of a big city constitutes the entire experience of a foreign country. I prefer to rent a car and drive through the land and into the rural countryside for me to feel I've seen a foreign nation. It's the earth energies I like to experience, not merely the people vibrations.

But earth and people sometimes combine to create islands of energy within a town or countryside. I was talking with John, a friend of mine, about this chapter, and he said, "I have a story to share with you."

Although retired now, John worked most of his life as a librarian, working in the city of Oakland, California. During one phase of his life, he was transferred to the Chinatown branch of the library system. "It was fascinating to walk to the library. I'd be walking down the street when all of a sudden, I would cross some invisible dividing line into Chinatown. The energized atmosphere totally changed into the 'Chinatown energy.' It was very palpable. And it was the same way going back to my car in the evening. I'd cross a certain street, and I'd be back in 'regular Oakland.'"

There is like a bubble in the middle of Oakland. That specialized etheric field is not only created by the sanskaras of the Asian people who live and work there, but I believe the energies of the earth itself also support and allow the Chinatown neighborhood to thrive at that specific locale and not in any other spot.

I live in a suburban community outside San Francisco. I have a house that backs up against eighteen hundred acres of open-space land, undeveloped parkland. My wife and I thrive on the supportive energies of nature—plants, rocks, and animals—while still being only ten minutes from downtown Walnut Creek. Many of my spiritual companions live in apartments near our Sufi Sanctuary. They trade the nature energy that I seem to require for the proximity to the living force coming from our beautiful domed building.

We've discussed the geographical spot on the globe where we live and the different energies of city versus suburb, and even the quality of energy in your neighborhood. Next, we examine the etheric energy component of interior design. There are many, many facets to this topic, and I will not pretend to be thorough in my discussion.

Let me set the stage for this consideration of interior design by quoting my friend Sri Aurobindo: "It is very true that physical things have a consciousness within them which feels in response to care and is sensitive to careless touch and rough handling. To know or feel that and learn to be careful of them is a great progress of consciousness." And another of his quotations: "There is a consciousness in physical things which is not the life and consciousness of man and animal which we know, but still secret and real. That is why we must have a respect for physical things and use them rightly, not misuse and waste ill-treatment or handle with a careless roughness. This feeling of all being conscious or alive comes when our own physical consciousness—and not the mind only—awakes out of its obscurity and becomes aware of the One in all things, the Divine everywhere" (Sri Aurobindo, *A Practical Guide to Integral Yoga,* p 266).

The interior design topic that first comes to my mind is feng shui, the Chinese science of placement and design. First, the feng shui expert notices how the house is situated on the earth and how that naturally affects its chi, or etheric energy. There is a house down the road from me that I always notice. As I drive by, the road seems to head straight for the house and then, at the last minute, curves sharply to the right. In feng shui, this would be referred to as "killer chi." According to their theories, etheric energy flows with cars along streets (also along rivers, streams, power lines, etc.). So, in this particular case, the chi doesn't always successfully make the turn in the road and runs right into the ill-positioned house. A feng shui practitioner might attribute illness, mental confusion, turmoil, or even divorce to the constant bombardment of killer chi. The cure for such an unfortunate house placement might be to install a mirror in front of the house to deflect the bad energy.

Some of my friends are not interested in such feng shui theories or "cures," because they say it sounds like magic. I say, "Exactly!" What is true magic other than the conscious manipulation of occult forces for practical reasons? Magic doesn't have to have a negative connotation. After all, every act of human kindness or love is true magic.

So according to the philosophy of the black hat, tantra sect of Tibetan Buddhism, you superimpose a geometric shape called a *bagua* over your house. Each wall or area or room of the house has a connection with one of eight areas of psychological life. The house, in a sense, becomes a picture of your life and personality. Thus, one corner represents "relationships and marriage." Another area represents "health." Another, "career," and so forth. If your career is faltering or uncertain, you place a particular cure in that portion of the house, or even portion of the property around the house. To stimulate or stabilize the career area, you could plant a tree in that corner of the yard or make a rock garden or fountain. In the house, you could hang a faceted crystal from the ceiling or position a plant or statue in the correct area. All these would have different magical effects on your career.

In my own life, I remember a time when our marriage was going through a rough patch. I took a two-hour feng shui seminar and ended up moving my bed to a new position in the bedroom and then put in a ficus tree behind it. Whether or not the feng shui cures worked is almost irrelevant. Taking action to help my marriage in such a concrete way gave me hope and confidence. And such feelings, all by themselves, created a new flow of energy in the relationship.

Of course, feng shui is a vast and fascinating topic, and my cursory examination cannot in any way do justice to the topic. In this discussion, I only wanted to introduce the subject; if this interests you, you can pursue the subject more fully.

Much of interior design and the energy you create in a home is reflected in the colors you choose for walls, floors, and furniture. Each color and shade holds and emits unseen energy. Cool colors, like blues and violets, tend to carry a calming influence, whereas hot colors—oranges and yellows—tend to have a more active feel. My meditation room, for example, is painted a light violet. I find that color helpful for meditating. When I added a garden room to my home, which is a south-facing room looking out on the garden, I painted it a bright coronation gold. Stepping into the room on a sunny day had a very revitalizing effect on my psyche. As Alla Svirinskaya says in her book, *Energy Secrets,*

> Colors affect our bodies in very specific ways. Color is the expression of the vital, generative life force of light, the force that sustains us. What we perceive as a particular color is actually wavelengths of active moving energy. Each wavelength has its unique signature and characteristics that impact on us in specific ways. The colors around us are in constant interaction with our bodies, as well as with our [feelings] and emotions. (p. 28)

Colors affect the unseen, astral environment as well. I once read that a spook in a haunted house had his headquarters in a certain upstairs bedroom. This room would emit bangs, shouts, shuffling of feet, and movement of furniture. The owners of the house repainted the room in a soothing light blue. The psychic activities in that room immediately calmed down.

Meher Baba once recommended that some of his Western followers decorate their house in shades of orange, green, and yellow. He said that as the years go by, these colors would be more pleasing in very light, pastel shades.

Of course, using color is a very personal matter. To some, having orange furniture, let's say, would be ridiculous; while others would feel wonderfully nurtured surrounded by orange.

I think for spiritual students, the ideal would be to use pale colors in your environment. The most important colors are the internal ones generated by the mind and reflected in the astral aura. You wouldn't want the colors in the house to overpower your inner colors. White, therefore, can be a good solution. White provides the canvas for your own psychological painting. It gives you the neutral background so you can relax and be yourself.

Often, however, a cold white can be the solution to wall color without any inner thought process involved. Landlords often paint apartments white, and motel rooms are white so that no one can object. White with dark furniture can feel very impersonal.

Many of my friends use a warmer, creamy white as a foundation for an interior statement. Often, cabinets, rugs, and furniture will be white or off-white. Also, you can introduce pale peach colors or soft greens as an accent. The effect of a mostly white room is very dramatic and appealing.

My murshid, Jim MacKie, was fond of celadon green in his decor. Celadon is a turquoise shade with more yellow. Green, in general, has a healing quality. Green crystals, for example, are said to stimulate physical vitality. I have had celadon wall-to-wall carpets in my home for thirty years. It's such a pleasing color, you never get tired of it. And it is very harmonious with creamy white walls.

Naturally, the shape of rooms has an energetic effect, too. Dr. Steiner developed a type of architecture called "organic architecture." In this building style, there is often a creative and harmonious interaction between angles and curves. Windows and doors and rooms are not rectangular but rather a combination of obtuse angles and curves. Dr. Steiner suggested that such forms help keep the energy in the space moving, and that energy can get stopped and blocked in the corners of a rectangular or square room. He used to say, "The devil hides in the corners." The angles in his architecture arise out of the mineral kingdom, whereas the curvy forms come from the plant kingdom.

I was fortunate enough to be great friends with the well-known anthroposophical artist, Maulsby Kimball. In 1978, Kim designed the garden room addition to my house. One of the features of the room is a bay window composed of three curvy windows and a window seat with harmonious angular molding framing the seat. People are stunned by the beauty of this room and always choose to sit and visit in that special space. The flowing energy of the room is palpable.

Cleanliness and clutter are also energy factors in a home. Just as you wash sanskaras off after being in public spaces, sanskaras and dirt accumulate in a house and need to be cleansed. Sanskaras and energy vibrations collect on your shoes, for example, and you carry the vibrations right into your home. That's why many cultures support the custom of leaving your shoes outside the door of the house. Mosques and Hindu temples, of course, do not allow shoes, either.

My first murshida used to tell her students that in cities and commercial areas, there is a one- or two-foot-high layer of unpleasant astral energy nearest the ground. Just as sand and debris settle on the bottom of a fish tank, so the most coarse and gross vibrations of greed, selfishness, and anger sink and build up closest to the ground. So if you walk down a city street, astral sludge can accumulate on your shoes and legs. Murshida also advised us not to put our mattresses on the ground so as to avoid sleeping in this "astral wash." Of course, this was Berkeley in the 1960s. Having your mattress on the floor (or multiple mattresses) was quite trendy in Berkeley, as was a lot of experimentation with drugs. As I'll explain in my chapter on drugs, use of mind-altering substances can attract an array of unpleasant astral currents. So drug vibes also accumulate in the astral wash.

Even at a shopping mall, the astral wash can be a couple of feet up from the ground. How often have you seen a young baby crying his head off while being wheeled in a stroller at a mall? Well, he's being wheeled through thick astral mud; no wonder he's crying.

Naturally, cleaning kitchen or bathroom floors and vacuuming rugs removes stagnant etheric energy and brightens the vibrations of a home. If dust and dirt are unpleasant to have around on the physical plane, just think how nasty the astral counterpart of dustiness appears. And if the house can be a metaphor for your own inner world, keeping the house clean can go a long way towards cleansing the mind and freeing it from binding, narrowing stresses and worries. Clutter around the home can also clog energy flow and accumulate etheric debris. The principles of feng shui teach us to keep sparkling energy flowing in a house by arranging furniture in certain ways, keeping the house clean, and removing clutter.

I find straightening up the house, removing old mail or magazines, or doing the dishes increases my personal energy and makes the house feel happy. Clutter, therefore, has psychological effect as well. Items left lying around the house in a haphazard manner hold energy, and as we walk by them, they attract our attention. Many such cluttering items attract an increasing amount of sensory attention, and pretty soon, our whole mental outlook can seem scattered and confused. When working on this book, for example, a straightened-up environment helps me use all my mental force to concentrate on my writing. My attention is not scattered or pulled this way and that.

Even if you need certain items close at hand, the excess, distracting energy is cut off by putting them away in closets, drawers, or closed cabinets. Out of sight, out of mind. Or if you cannot see something, the energy link between you and it is cut off. That's another way to look at it: Visible clutter simply saps your energy. Think of a stack of mail lying around, maybe even unopened. As you walk by the stack, you might think, *How am I going to pay that dental bill?* or *I have to answer this letter to Grandma.* As the occult principle goes, "Energy follows thought." Dealing with the stack of mail or putting it in a drawer helps conserve personal energy.

I knew a spiritual person who discussed an aspect of his spiritual unfoldment with me. During a particular phase, he could hear books. Every book carries its own sanskaras, plus the impressions of the author who wrote it. This person's experience was hearing each book as a talk show on the radio. He could actually hear the impressions within each book. Library books hold even more complex patterns of impressions because each reader also psychically imprints the book. So when this man went into a library or bookstore, it would be as if each book was tuned to a different radio frequency that whispered (or yelled) the book's contents. This spiritual teacher found in his own home that putting his personal library behind doors in attractive cabinets kept the book vibrations down to a minimum. Books talked to him, and they were noisy. The cabinets quieted everything.

On a more material level, we all live in confusing cross currents of electromagnetic radiation from our wireless communication devices. It's not surprising that some electro-hypersensitive people can't sleep in apartments where different Wi-Fi frequencies are continually bombarding their consciousness from apartments to the left and right, above and below (see the technology chapter).

Thankfully, there are ways to shield and protect yourself from electromagnetic radiation, just as there are ways to protect your aura from unpleasant psychic vibrations—especially in the home. Attractive colors and furniture with lots of light in rooms, and a maximum of cleanliness and a minimum of clutter, create a very pleasant psychic atmosphere.

Some impressions can haunt an environment, and they can be much trickier to clean. We all live in apartments and houses that had previous occupants. And these occupants left their psychic residue all through the house. Their sanskaras cannot be removed with just soap and water.

The first principle, in my opinion, is to be very careful when seeking new living accommodations. When you walk into an apartment or house, you will usually get an immediate first impression of the psychic environment. If the place doesn't feel like home, don't move in. It doesn't matter how great a deal it is financially. It's not worth dealing with the headache of purifying or cleansing the psychic atmosphere. Perhaps a couple lived there before who argued a lot and had a contentious marriage. Perhaps an alcoholic or a heavy drug user lived there. Or maybe someone died on the property or even committed suicide. These concerns are not merely topics found in scary movies. They're real. It's just like the police in the movies, looking through the rooms of a house for a bad guy and yelling, "Clear!" You need a place where you can say, "Clear."

I remember when I was looking for a house to buy in 1974. My realtor would pick me up every Tuesday after school to look at various properties. Some houses I saw had such a dark astral atmosphere, it felt like a vise had gripped my head the moment I walked through the front door. You don't even need to look into the causes of such an atmosphere. If you're at all sensitive psychically, you'll feel the vibe. Just get out.

The house I ended up buying was the house of a widower whose family had grown up and moved away. But the old man invited neighborhood children to play on his property. He even built a playhouse in the backyard for the neighborhood kids. He died in the house, yet his soul force had definitely moved on into bright realms of the astral. The house was a happy, clear environment.

If for some reason you end up living in a space that isn't happy or clear, you can always spiritually cleanse the rooms. I remember one dear friend who ended up in a haunted house in Marin County in the Bay Area. She frequently could see the spooks sitting on a doorframe or other improbable places. She was advised to put cut-out, five-pointed stars on the lintels of every door. Then, one night during a particularly creepy visitation, she yelled at the spooks, "In the name of Avatar Meher Baba, all spirits depart!" There was a noisy, windy, whirling sound, like you might hear in an aviary if the birds were startled. Then silence. The ghosts were gone for good.

There are so many other ways of cleansing stagnant, astral sludge from a house. You can try meditation or visualizations of the house perking up and sparkling in golden light. You can ring bells or burn incense in the rooms, perhaps while reciting a personally sacred mantra. Candles also can help, or sacred statues, say, of spiritual figures. I read that putting a piece of copper pipe in the corners of a room helps keep the room psychically clean.

And for goodness sakes, try not to bring unpleasantness into the house after you move in. Used furniture and especially antiques often hold more than artistic appeal. Folks with the psychic sense of psychometry can feel impressions of the builder of a piece of furniture and also tune into all the folks who have owned the piece. Everything is a databank of past sanskaras, and an antique can hold unlucky or even cursed vibrations merely by having been owned by unpleasant people.

The only real-life example I know of, concerning antiques, is about a ring. A friend of mine purchased an old jeweled ring at an auction. After she started wearing the ring, her health deteriorated. She got chronic fatigue-like symptoms that would not resolve themselves. Her mother knew a psychic and asked why her daughter's health had so recently taken a tailspin. The psychic said, "It's the old ring." The ring, it turned out, had belonged to an unhappy and sickly lady who had committed suicide while wearing it. The psychic said to dispose of the ring in a way no one else could ever be harmed by the vibrations of its energy. The daughter threw it into the middle of a lake. Her health issues immediately improved.

Of course, the opposite can be true as well. A chair, let's say, used by a spiritual master can offer a steady stream of rose-colored radiance to a room and lift the spirits of all who come near it.

In this chapter, I discussed the inner side of the environment in which we live. Everything has an occult influence: all the way from the portion of the earth we call home to the direction our house faces. It's fun to try to be aware of these influences, to be consciously conscious of them. Creating glowing, positive, uplifting environments at home and at work can have a tremendous effect on your moods and on your health. And stand up for your rights to a pure environment. If friends take you to a bar that feels unpleasant, politely excuse yourself. If you are shown to a motel room that repels you, or even one that smells bad, ask for a different room. If you consciously try to purify the atmosphere wherever you go, you can find homes everywhere on Mother Earth.

CHAPTER 5
The World of Thoughts

Our mind is like a market place; we don't realize it, but we could
hardly call one thought out of a hundred our own, bathing
as we do in the whirling sea of thoughts all around us.
—Georges van Vrekhem (*The Mother,* 2012, p 450)

Up until this chapter, I have emphasized that energies from so-called
subjective realms of the inner planes can be felt objectively through
sensitized physical senses. Now we move on to perhaps the most powerful
of spiritual energies that in this physical world are expressed entirely
subjectively: the world of thoughts. We simply think the thoughts that
are in us and around us. However, even thoughts can be surprisingly
objective on the astral plane, and thoughts present us with a significant
topic of study.

The Buddha once said, "We are nothing but a bundle of thoughts."
And for many human beings, the sense of "I" or ego or personality is really
dictated by the contents of the thinking mind. Even Descartes said, "I
think, therefore I am." But what do thoughts have to do with the occult
energies discussed in this book?

Thought energy is definitely different from the etheric currents you
feel in living things, minerals, or sacred places around the globe. But
thoughts are nonetheless a form of energy from the invisible realms, only
this type of energy we experience subjectively as the content of our heads.

What are thoughts? Let me try to articulate my understanding of them
from fifty years of studying and research. I included a chapter in *The Secret
Life of Kids* on thought transference back in 1987. Obviously, thoughts

originate and are stored in mental sanskaras on the mental planes. In the mental world, thoughts and ideas exist as delicate traces of light. The coded fibers of mind are in a partially expressed aggregate of sanskaras in the subtle body when a soul incarnates on the earth. A thought sanskara can be stimulated from internal means (i.e., from other sanskaras) or from external means connected with the subtle, astral, or physical environment.

A sanskara stimulated in the subtle body gives off a vibration and is pumped up with force and energy and is then caught by the brain. The electrical charges of the neurons give rise to the perception of a thought. During this almost instantaneous process, that particular vibration or frequency of the thought passes through astral matter. "Like attracts like" is a spiritual law. Astral matter vibrating to the same frequency coagulates around the original vibration, and if the thought is strong or often repeated, it gathers shape and color in astral matter and becomes what is called in spiritual and occult literature a "thought form." A thought form is what you might call the incarnation of that delicate, mental trace as it vibrates and manifests in the astral world.

Once a thought form is manifest, it can easily replicate its content in the thinker by directly stimulating the physical sanskaras connected to nerve tissue in the brain. A thought form can bounce in and out of your aura or even find a rather permanent existence stuck to your etheric brain. Each time the thought is activated, it in turn gets a recharge and is pumped up with more astral prana, and its form and color are intensified.

But beyond that, your energized thought form can now influence others. And it can even be sent off to purposely affect the astral environment. David Spangler, in his book *Subtle Worlds,* describes thought forms this way:

> If you invest [a thought] image with enough emotional and mental energy, particularly in the form of desire and will, you can propel that image out of your personal subtle field into the subtle energies of the imaginal [astral] realm.
>
> At that point it becomes a thought form. Under the right circumstances, it can detach from you and gain a semiautonomous existence, assuming it can draw energy from somewhere else to sustain it. If someone else draws

that thought form into their personal subtle field, they might find themselves suddenly and unaccountably thinking [that thought].

Of course, Spangler adds, most thoughts "dissolve fairly quickly and certainly never get beyond the aura of the person who created it" (quoted with the author's permission).

The parapsychologist Charles Tart, in his book *The End of Materialism,* says that sending thoughts from person to person, through astral membranes, is a process that has been proven through scientific experimentation to be real. This phenomenon is called telepathy. In my earlier book, I defined telepathy simply as "the ability to receive the thoughts and feelings of others." It's one of the seven major psychic abilities or psychic senses. Though we've all had certain telepathic experiences, like knowing who's on the phone when it rings or voicing the unspoken thought of a spouse, testimony from telepaths decidedly proves that thoughts are everywhere, and they are things.

Thoughts are astral things that are objective, coalesced vibrating fields that can travel from person to person.

In my other book, I tell the story of Linda, who was very telepathic as a child. This ability was tremendously annoying because she had no control over the thoughts she would "hear." She couldn't turn the ability on or off. The only way she could get away from the impinging world of thoughts was to escape into nature or play with her Down's syndrome friend who was "clear." Today, Linda still recollects how the occult energies of thought vibrations disrupted her entire childhood. Linda told me her hypersensitivity was like having her skin peeled off, so the intensity of every passing breeze or change of temperature was not from the physical world, but from the thought world.

Interactions with people were the most problematic. Linda heard what people said and saw what they did, and she was aware at the same time of what they were really thinking and feeling. And these often didn't match up. As a child, I remember having to kiss and hug my great-aunt Violet. She was a fat, unpleasant woman with a prickly mustache. I remember kissing and hugging her while being inwardly repulsed at the same time. Thank goodness Aunt Vi wasn't telepathic. For Linda, interactions with people "were a confusing jumble of conflicting impressions, resulting in a breakdown of communications and extreme sensory overload" (*The Secret Life of Kids*).

Her earliest memory was the frightening impression that her own mother, though outwardly nurturing and loving, inwardly rejected her and in fact felt antipathy toward her. Her mother was a proper English lady, married to a red-headed, hot-tempered Irishman. After the birth of their first and well-loved daughter, she hoped her second child would be a blond and blue-eyed English boy. Instead, Linda turned out to be a replica of her father: fiery, red-headed, Irish in every way, and the wrong sex.

Linda's mother seemed never to get over her bitter disappointment. Every time she said something nice to Linda and reached out to pick her up, Linda shrank because she felt her mother was really repulsed by her. This telepathic information was clearer than any words.

These impressions Linda felt during her childhood were not based on words. She said these impulses she picked up were a combination of thoughts and feelings. She was receptive to such thought-feelings.

I mentioned how this lonely little girl could escape her cluttered astral life by going out into nature. Here, the hills surrounding her home and even her mother's garden offered her a sanctuary of soothing, reliable, and truthful nature energies. She could tune out the anxieties, stress, and fear caused by her social world. Animals also gave her great happiness. She had an adorable pet cat. The birds, squirrels, and other wildlife around her home also radiated pleasant energies. She remembers how she could tune into the energies of wildlife. She often could do things like walk right up to a tree where a bobcat was napping.

Today, Linda loves to knit animals, especially bunnies and horses and unicorns. When we discuss gardening in another chapter, I'll mention how each type of flower radiates a different energy that carries different divine forces. Linda, as a child, could also feel these messages of the flowers. Today, she has the most spectacular garden of any of my friends. She has a true green thumb. Plus, she has a knack of attracting the fairy folk.

Elementary school turned out to be a nightmare for Linda. Hearing the thoughts of the other children kept her from focusing on her schoolwork. She remembers taking tests and picking up the confusion of the other students. She was hardly able to concentrate because she had to continually sift out her own knowledge from the astral static coming from all around her. It was like other students had their own psychic radio that was tuned to a different frequency. Once Linda came into the classroom, she would hear all her classmates' radios at once. No wonder she yearned to escape into nature.

Of course, like most psychic children, Linda assumed that everyone could tune into the same astral currents as she did. She was always astonished that everybody else seemed to cope so effortlessly with a crowded social environment like the school classroom, when for her, the negativity and anger of others was literally painful. It wasn't until high school that Linda finally learned that other people relied almost exclusively on words for communication. She had always felt that words were unreliable.

One can easily imagine that high school was even more problematic. Linda shared an enlightening anecdote with me: Once, during her teen years, she was walking on the sidewalk near a movie theater. A group of adolescent boys were approaching from the other direction. Linda could feel their explosive lust energy and surging, unrestrained, almost primal ego forces. The thought form smashed into her, and she quickly ran to the other side of the street to get out of the undulating energy field of adolescent sexual force. Thoughts are things.

My wife, Hana, has an infant memory similar to Linda's. Hana was in her crib, dressed in a onesie when her father stepped into the room, smoking a cigarette. He was a country singer and frequently did concerts on the road with his band. Hana remembers him thinking, *Gosh, I'm glad I have a daughter, and I'm glad there were no birth complications. But I have a gig and wish I could leave and go on the road.*

It wasn't Hana's infant brain that picked up the thought energies and translated them. To my way of thinking, she was conscious of a portion of her mind that had not yet fully incarnated into her infant form.

Much later in life, Hana had a vivid experience of the energies I call thought forms. She was in a dramatic musical presentation, in which she had several singing solos. Weeks before her performance, she had a lot of difficulty sleeping due to her worries about the show. In fact, Hana identified her feelings as worry, fear, and dread. Apparently, these three thought-feelings were so omnipresent for her, she pumped them up with psychic energy and created living, vibrant thought forms.

Her performance went very well, and she never missed a note. The night before the last show, she was feeling relief and gratitude for a job well done. She was filled with a golden light. Suddenly, she saw three dark forms moving toward her. They were a lot like shadows with moving, flexible tendrils reaching out every which way. They were headed for their usual resting place in the nets of Hana's etheric body. Hana remembers sending out this message: *No, I don't feel that way anymore. Go away.* The golden light of her aura pulsed, and the thought forms of worry, fear, and dread disappeared.

My late teacher, Murshid MacKie, used to say that thoughts and feelings are made of astral "tissue," and they had shape, color, flexible energy, and edges. People attract certain of these vibrational thoughts and feelings, and they attach themselves to their "nets of consciousness." When this happens, people feel the feelings and think the thoughts and automatically absorb the energy into their personality: "Those are my thoughts. They are part of me." The process was somewhat humorous to Murshid because he could easily see that particular thought-feeling had originated outside the thinker and was just drifting by on a flowing, astral current.

The astral world, however, is cluttered with thought debris floating in endless currents. Becoming conscious of this debris is helpful because some energy is positive and some is negative. Here is an anecdote that illustrates how important it is to understand these astral thought energies. In the early years of my teaching career, I thought it would be nice to take my class on a field trip to the local police department. It's never too soon to demonstrate to children that police officers are your friends and helpers.

All was going well, and the tour was very informative. Then the tour guide showed the children the little holding cell where prisoners would be placed in between the booking process and the assignment of a more permanent jail accommodation. The cell was probably eight feet by eight feet. One-third of my class of children could fit in it at a time. When my turn came, I knew I had made a mistake bringing the children here. The holding cell had very thick, oppressive, and disturbing qualities. I needed to get out of there fast.

When we were going back to the parents' cars, Stacy, an eight-year-old girl I knew was clairvoyant, ran up to me and said, "Mr. Peterson, do you want me to tell you what I saw in that jail cell?"

"No," I replied, "but when we get back to class, draw me a picture." I still have the crayon drawing Stacy drew of the thought forms she saw in the jail. There was a mass of jagged lightning bolts made of black and red light, with smaller black and red squiggles wiggling in between the several jagged forms. You can imagine the continually refreshed thought-feelings of prisoners in that cell: hatred, anger, resentment, violence, fear: lightning bolts of unpleasantness.

Because of me, the children all drenched their innocent auras into that terrible psychic storm. I'm sure some were injured by the violent thought forms. I can only hope the guardian angels of the kids protected them. But I learned my lesson. I never took children on a field trip to the police station ever again.

In 1909, Dr. Annie Besant, the Theosophical Society president, said in a lecture, what's the good of a spiritual student knowing all about the inner laws of the unseen worlds if "he does not utilize his knowledge to his own helping and to the helping of those around him?" (*Invisible Worlds*, p 219). That's truly the focus of this entire book: learning how the energies of the invisible planes impinge on us all the time and therefore learning how to take them into account in daily life.

Let's examine some scenarios from the perspective of the world of thoughts. Imagine you're in a large mall or indoor shopping center. What are the thought forms that fill such a structure? First of all, because the focus is shopping and buying, the thought forms would be of specific types, and they would be strong. Every day, a new batch of shoppers would add their psychic energy to the existing forms, not only pumping them up energetically, but also giving the thought forms almost an autonomous existence, endowing them with a life of their own. In fact, it is said, small elemental astral beings can even inhabit thought patterns. The thoughts in a mall also could be light and happy, from people window-shopping or having a snack. But just as often, shoppers could be in a rush, greedy to get to the store with the most sale items or selfish with the passion to accumulate new shoes or a new coat. Also, there are the children who are whining, "Buy me this," or "I'm hungry."

For sensitive people, the indoor shopping mall can be a very unpleasant place, indeed. For children and infants, it can even be psychically dangerous. In the environment chapter, I discussed the astral wash; that's the heavy astral energy that descends and clings to streets, sidewalks, and floors. Well, much of that toxic layer is composed of thought forms. And the walls and the ceilings of a mall bottle up the accumulated astral force (walls exist on the astral level too). The whole place becomes what I like to call a psychic pressure cooker. It's not an accident children get so cranky at shopping malls.

The way I survive at shopping malls is to wear dark glasses; sometimes, I hold a pocket crystal in my left hand and mentally recite a mantra (mine is my master's name: Meher Baba). I try to stay focused. If I need a pair of jeans, I go to the correct department in the correct store, and I don't allow my mind to get into a passive state, taking in the sights. That way, the passing thoughts of others don't have a chance to stick on me.

In my hometown, Walnut Creek, we have a very delightful outdoor mall called Broadway Plaza. The outside fountains, trees, and flowers dramatically mitigate the nasty feelings that can bombard you in an indoor mall. Buying a pair of jeans can be a happy experience, instead of running a psychic gauntlet.

Movie theaters can be a den of thought forms, as well. As I have become more sensitive through the years, I find the movie theater experience less and less appealing. There's a movie story I heard forty years ago that I've never forgotten. Paul, a friend of mine who is wide open psychically, went to see the new release, *The Exorcist*. He said the theater was swarming with thoughts of fear and shock, and many elemental entities were frolicking in and among the thought forms. One nasty little thought creature stuck to Paul's aura and came home with him. Paul said it was a day or two before he could get rid of that dark, little imp.

Bars can also be hotspots for picking up bad thoughts. In bars, there is also the danger of being affected by discarnate human beings who were alcoholics in their earth life days. They hang out in bars to overshadow drinkers and at least get the aroma of the alcohol. I think the British model of a pub is a much more appealing place from the occult point of view. The lights are not as dim as in American bars, a fire might be lit in the fireplace, and people might be playing darts. And whole families might be enjoying a bit of dinner. The thought forms in such an establishment would be much happier.

Obviously, there are plenty of places to find mellow and happy thoughts in the psychic atmosphere. You can find sanctuary from an overcrowded world of thoughts anywhere in nature: deserts, oceanside, mountains, or simply a favorite park. As Linda said earlier, in nature the atmosphere is "clear." Cities are way more densely packed with people's thought energies than the countryside. I mostly avoid cities, unless I'm going to a concert or play. The crowds of thought forms can be worse than the crowds of people. However, thoughts are energy, and many people love the wonderfully diverse energies of city life. They thrive in cities.

When I was in my twenties, I interviewed clairvoyant children. Those children all saw geometric shapes in the air when out in nature. They saw stars, squares, triangles floating nets, all sorts of things, but I'm not really sure what they signify. Speaking of shapes, there's one interesting piece of information I collected during my research for *The Secret Life of Kids*. When dogs bark, they apparently spew out a projectile that appears as a red- or orange-colored missile. It's pointed at the end and zips through space twenty feet or so, depending on the size or strength of the dog. No wonder some people are bothered by the bark of dogs. They get hit by an energized torpedo.

It's easy to find oases of pleasant thoughts. Any religious temple would be a sanctuary for peaceful thought forms. Most restaurants, museums, and art galleries are happy places. Concert halls, where music is played, hold a very different vibration from the movie theater's vibration. You can easily be guided by intuition. Also, you carry your own thought atmosphere with you all the time. You and a group of friends can influence the thought world wherever you go. You can bring happiness and love with you.

In the chapter on water, I discussed how words, music, and even thoughts can affect and alter the crystalline structure of water. Thoughts can alter physical matter. The ancient Avatar, Zoroaster, was not merely giving symbolic or ethical advice when he said that the foundation of the spiritual life is "good thoughts, good words, and good deeds." It's important to remember that the thoughts we think and dwell on influence the world around us, both the psychic world and the material world.

I wanted to conclude this chapter on the world of thoughts with a startling anecdote from my own master, Meher Baba. A telepath once went to Baba's headquarters to test him. A fake master who pretended to be enlightened would surely show his real colors directly in his thoughts. So this man wanted to prove that Baba was not who people thought he was.

The man sat down in front of the amused Baba, closed his eyes, and concentrated on Baba's mind. He could pick up absolutely no thoughts coming from the master.

"Why can't I read your mind and pick up your thoughts?" asked the man.

"Because I have no mind," said Baba.

That's what it means to be God realized: The normal sanskaras that create the lower mind of thinking and feeling do not exist.

CHAPTER 6

Sacred Pilgrimage: In Search of the Miraculous

Travel has always been a reliable technique to recoup my energies and replenish the occult reservoir of etheric force. Sometimes, a sluggish life force can be stimulated by the sights and sounds of a new place or foreign land, very much the way acupuncture can stimulate the body's chi. Merely taking myself out of the regular, workaday world can be very energetically rejuvenating as well.

From the spiritual point of view, a traveler's destination has great significance. And if you head for a site with deep inner personal meaning, recharging your etheric batteries can be the least of its effects. Inner transformation can occur. Being in a sacred site is like taking a shower in spiritual light. This force can mitigate the effects of unwanted sanskaras and leave the aspirant recharged and blessed. A journey to a sacred site is usually called a pilgrimage.

Some people feel the need to begin a spiritual quest, but they may be unable to contact the inner source of their quest deep within. The path of spirituality involves finding the inner self. In early stages of this quest, finding spiritual stimulation in the outer world can kick-start the real inner journey. A true pilgrimage in the outer world can be a great help in awakening the inner being of the seeker.

There are four basic sacred sites that you can head to in your pilgrimage. The first is a completely natural place. Some natural formations created by air, earth, water, or fire through the workings of Mother Earth hold tremendous occult force. The first two that come to my mind are California's Mount Shasta and the red rocks of Sedona, Arizona.

The second type of sacred destination is where people have placed markers to stimulate and amplify Mother Earth's natural forces. These are places like Stonehenge and Salisbury Cathedral, a building purposely built on a powerful chakra of the earth.

The third is a human-made structure sanctified and charged over the years by its form, by its use, or simply by all the people who have worshiped at the site and honored it. Examples of this type of structure would be the Kaaba, in Mecca, or the Great Pyramid in Egypt.

Finally, some sacred sites are made holy by spiritual figures: saints, masters, or adepts of the past or present. Immediately, a spot in central India comes to mind. It's called the Valley of the Saints, near a town called Khuldabad. The tombs of seven hundred saints and masters lie in this lush valley. To enter the valley, without even visiting the tombs, is an amazing experience.

So let's now analyze these four types of pilgrimage areas to better understand their significance and the origins of their unique power. Our worldly mother gives us energy, nutrition, and a feeling of well-being, not only when we are young children, but sometimes well into adult life. Our Mother Earth can do the same. A pilgrimage is a quest for inner spiritual sources, accomplished by going out into the world. A sacred site is a place in the outer world that creates an inner awakening, strengthens your inner link to life's forces, and stimulates that subjective energy that manifests as love and intuition. But how do we find and recognize these special places?

The earth is a living being and has currents of telluric or earth force running in lines crisscrossing the planet. Some are positively charged, and some are negatively charged. Human beings also have meridians throughout the physical body, concentrated at special energy nodes called chakras. Spiritual teachers can recognize such vital centers, psychics can feel them, and dowsers can detect them with dowsing instruments.

To locate such centers on the earth, however, you don't have to be psychic or spiritually advanced; people have recognized such sites and worshiped at them for thousands of years. They're often characterized by unusual geographic features: a very tall mountain, a volcano, an unusual rock formation, a cave, or a natural spring; lakes, rivers, and waterfalls are other possibilities. I've always felt very sensitive to cave energy. Psychiatrist Jean Brolin says that caves are symbolic wombs or tombs. If you descend into a cave, an opening into Mother Earth, you are entering a symbolic journey into the underworld or the "other world, the place from which all life comes and to which all life returns in death" (*Crossing to Avalon*, p 75).

I've been to many caves in California. But recently, I had an especially energetic experience in Maui, Hawaii. My wife and I were in Wai'anapanapa State Park near Hana. We walked to a cave filled with fresh water, although near the ocean. I couldn't resist jumping into the ice-cold water and exploring the cave. I swam back into room after room until I could barely see the light at the cave mouth in the distance. I was in ecstasy. I felt so energized. Something about this blending of water and rock was so filled with force. I even meditated on a rocky ledge, despite the cold water. Meditation is always a good way to try to unite with whatever telluric force you feel at a sacred earth site. Anyhow, by the time I emerged from this cave, I was tingling with etheric energy. My eyes and aura were radiating with happiness. My experience inside that water cave was the high point of my weeklong Hawaiian trip, a week with so many high points.

Another cave experience that is embedded in my memory was the crystal cave on the island of Staffa, near the holy island of Iona, Scotland. Fingal's Cave is reached by boat from Iona, and it is another water cave. You walk on a narrow ledge around the island from the boat ramp. Entering this cave, a magical sight awaits, with emerald-green water splashing in and out. The cave is formed of massive basalt hexagonal columns. It's truly the archetypal crystal cave. I was almost knocked over by the spiritual force. I found a secluded spot and meditated to tune into the amazing energies. But I had to rely on breathing to unite with the sacred earth energies because I couldn't keep my eyes closed. I just was mesmerized by the awesome thirty-foot crystal pillars. Much later, I went to see the basalt columns at the Devils Postpile in California. But that remarkable mountain couldn't begin to compare with the magical experience of Fingal's Cave.

I could fill an entire volume with experiences I've had making sacred pilgrimages around the world to natural wonders of our Mother Earth. But I think I've described this type of pilgrimage fully enough. Whenever you need to recharge your psychic battery or escape the human-made world of stress and strain, simply head for a known spot in nature that is spoken of in local traditions as being sacred or particularly beautiful. The experience of beauty itself holds tremendous spiritual force. Any travel, locally or internationally, can be enlivened by including some spiritual destinations into your itinerary.

Now let's turn our attention to my second type of sacred site. During the decade from 1995 to 2005, my son, Blake, and I started journeying to international destinations each summer. It turned out the British Isles became our favorite stomping grounds, particularly because we both felt very strongly that we had had past lifetimes in England and particularly in Scotland. Also, there were lots of exciting sacred sites to visit: Findhorn Gardens, New Grange, Glastonbury, Tintagel, and on and on. But I had a bit of an obsession that guided more than a few of our summer adventures. I love stone circles. During our visits to England, Ireland, and Scotland, we visited sixty-five stone circles.

Stone circles are examples of my second category of sacred sites. They are spots where telluric currents from Mother Earth are very strong, but also have been marked and amplified by human efforts. A discussion about occult geography, sometimes called geomancy, is important at this point.

According to tradition and various modern investigators, such as John Mitchell, earth is crisscrossed by lines of etheric energy, somewhat like the human body has lines of chi called meridians. Some of these energy currents have a positive or masculine charge, some have a negative charge, while some are balanced or neutral. In Britain, such a telluric grid is composed of ley lines. In ancient times (probably far more ancient than modern archeologists would admit), Druid sages and shamans had the ability to sense or even see these earth forces. Sometimes, ley lines would follow underground streams, sometimes a rocky ridge of a hill or mountain, and sometimes the straight tracks would simply zip across a meadow or valley, ending up at a hillock with a circle of trees, perhaps, or maybe charging a bubbling spring. It's too much to cite all the research into ley lines, so the reader will simply have to take my summaries as IMHO (in my humble opinion).

Anyway, by whatever psychic awareness was possessed by these ancient ones, they commemorated and celebrated and utilized these power currents in many ways. The markers they used to identify power spots were standing stones or stone circles. My favorite way to view the stones is that the shamans saw a place where a powerful negative current would intersect an equally forceful positive current. At such an intersection, an occult power point, node, or earth chakra would be created. Those ancient peoples erected circles of stones at these chakras, not only to mark the sights to be used for ritual purposes, but also to amplify the energies, which would be radiated into the surrounding valleys to support healthy livestock and crops and human growth. The upright stones work sort of like reversed lightning rods. The stone would attract the earth prana, channel it up, and radiate it out into the surrounding etheric atmosphere.

To locate the stone circles, I had a wonderful book called *A Guide to the Stone Circles of Britain, Ireland and Brittany*. With this book, my son and I located the largest rings, Stonehenge, Brodgar in Orkney, and the impressive Callanish Stones on the Isle of Lewis in Scotland. We also explored tiny stone circles way off the beaten track, a hundred yards into a wheat field. Blake, at nine or ten, could instantly feel the force of a ring. He would describe a particularly powerful ring as being like "an alien force field." The etheric energy would give you an electrical, tingling feeling all over your body. Entering certain stone rings, such as the huge Callanish Stones, some fifteen feet high, would be almost like passing into a new dimension or alternate universe. Blake also liked to locate the king stone, the focal point of the earth energies of the ring. He would touch each stone, close his eyes, and finally tell me, "Dad, this is the one."

Of course, some stone circles, Blake reported, were "duds." They seemed worn out and channeled none of the force we had experienced in other places. Perhaps, over the millennia, the ley lines had shifted. Or maybe these particular stones had simply stopped conducting etheric forces. Or possibly the circle never was potent. In some circles, I was literally forced to my knees in prayer, because they felt so strong. I would frequently try to do an extensive period of meditation, with my back up against the king stone. It felt like I was taking a magical and enlivening etheric shower.

To me, the earth energies released are almost materialized in an ancient stone circle and are as sacred as any spiritual force found in a temple, church, or sanctuary. They were wonderful places to visit and perfect spots to allow yourself to be rejuvenated by Mother Earth's loving caress.

There are many other spots where humans have purposely marked or amplified telluric power points. The first ones that come to mind are Machu Picchu in Peru, Glastonbury Abbey in England, and the famous Ellora Caves in India. Situated near Aurangabad in Maharashtra State, the Ellora Caves are in a valley brimming with energy. Hindus, Buddhists, and Jains carved stupendous temples into the rocky cliffs. The cave temples still are wonderful hotspots radiating divine force and blessings.

The third category of sacred sites are structures built by humans, often with religious significance, which have built up spiritual energies over the centuries, due to human devotion or awe. Baraka is a Sufi term for that spiritual force. It's a useful term, since a single word to identify the occult power found at certain sites doesn't exist in other esoteric traditions.

The Great Pyramid of Giza in Egypt tops my list of human-made sacred, energetic centers. The structure was never used as a tomb but was a temple of spiritual initiation. The baraka built up from these ancient rites over millennia, particularly in the King's Chamber, is palpable. Of course, the architectural design of the pyramid also collects spiritual force.

As I reported in *The Secret Life* of *Kids*, I went through a period when I experimented with pyramid shapes. I constructed an exact cardboard replica of the great pyramid and mounted it on top of a four-legged stand. I put it in the corner of my classroom, and students would lie on pillows and read in there. I called it the Reading Temple. Well, several clairvoyant children saw green and golden light radiating into the temple from the four corners of the pyramid. The planes of energy met in the middle and radiated, like a laser beam, starting at the apex and shooting into the floor. They also saw blue spheres of light, around eight inches in diameter, flow out of the top of the pyramid and drift up through the ceiling, kind of like etheric smoke signals.

The Reading Temple was a sought-after sanctuary, although a few children were actually repelled by its unfamiliar energies. A footnote to the discussion of the great pyramid is this unusual observation: When visiting the Giza Plateau, I surprisingly experienced more spiritual force near the Sphinx than inside the Great Pyramid. There is truly some beneficent force connected with that half-human monument.

Another unusually shaped spiritual sanctuary is the Kaaba in Mecca. Although I haven't experienced this force myself, millions of Muslims will attest to its rejuvenating, energizing, and inspiring power.

Another interesting building to visit is the Goetheanum, Rudolf Steiner's center for his Anthroposophical Society, in Switzerland. I have journeyed there twice. The story I wanted to tell about this structure, however, actually occurred some ninety-four years ago and concerns Steiner's first Goetheanum.

The first Goetheanum was a fabulous double-domed building, mostly built of carved wood. The majority of the building was completed in 1919 and was used for lectures and artistic performances. The Sufi saint who brought Sufism to America, Hazrat Inayat Khan, was living in France in 1920. One of his students suggested he must see Rudolf Steiner's architectural masterpiece. Murshid Khan liked the idea, so they drove to a hill where they had a clear view across the valley to the village of Dornach. There, perched on a hillside, was the Goetheanum. As Inayat Khan gazed at the structure through the eyes of a mental-plane master, he turned to his companion and said, "That building holds and conducts so much spiritual force, I don't know why it doesn't spontaneously burst into flames." The tragic thing was that less than two years later, an arsonist torched the Goetheanum, and it burned to the ground.

One pilgrimage site not associated with any edifice at all is one of my favorite human-made pilgrimage centers: the Findhorn Gardens. In the 1960s, Peter and Eileen Caddy and Dorothy MacLean began to communicate and cooperate with spiritual forces in the natural world. Working with the guidance of angelic and elemental consciousness, they began a remarkable community focused on a magical garden. This garden proved that cooperation with invisible life forces can manifest unexpected results, even in the inhospitable, sandy soil of northern Scotland. The divine energy you feel on entering the Findhorn Foundation community shows that human beings are the real channelers of invisible power.

And that brings me to our last category of sacred places of pilgrimage. If you really want to renew, expand, contemplate, and experience the great spiritual energies of life, you need to go to the tomb or the center sanctified and charged by the life and work of an authentic spiritual saint or master.

If ordinary human beings could create a Findhorn, just imagine what extraordinary people like, say, a St. Francis could create.

Advanced states of spiritual consciousness do not arise from a soul becoming good or wise or selfless. Rather, consciousness of the inner planes or of God, the goal and destiny of all living creatures, comes from the thinning out and annihilation of sanskaras. Sanskaras are the coded web of mental fibers that cover or obscure the vision of divine reality that is omnipresent.

As sanskaras are released and "unwound," the spiritual living energy locked in the sanskaras is unbound and radiated into the surrounding environment. This is why the aura of spiritually advanced beings is nothing but palpable radiating love. This radiant, energetic love permeates the headquarters of saints and masters and even radiates from the tomb where their bodies are buried.

The devotion and love from pilgrims who visit such a sacred site over the centuries amps up the energy and creates what Sufis call baraka or spiritual force. Such a charged atmosphere is not subtle, like some of the sacred sites discussed earlier, but can inundate an aspirant with a tidal wave of love, light, or bliss.

Visiting the home of Meher Baba or his tomb in India has always held miraculous experiences for me during these past forty-eight years. Each of my pilgrimages has been different. One energy experience I recall occurred in 1979 in Baba's tomb shrine. I was meditating in the tomb when it suddenly felt as though the base of my spine had been plugged into an electrical current. Overpowering energy started coursing up my spine. I became lightheaded and started to tingle all over with the strong prana. The plugged-in force flowed nonstop for around fifteen minutes. Then, just as suddenly, it stopped. I was unplugged.

During a 1975 visit to India, I went to the tomb of another great spiritual figure named Narayan Maharaj, who died in the 1940s. The spiritual atmosphere of his headquarters and tomb were fabulously charged. This time, it felt like I was walking into a force field of extreme peacefulness. Meditation consisted of closing my eyes and letting the currents of energy simply wash over me.

Narayan's last living direct disciple, Jiddu Krishnamurti, served me tea outdoors. He said, "When Maharaj was alive, this place was bustling.

Hundreds of people came every day. Now, just look; Kedgoan is empty. Don't people realize Maharaj's force is still here?" Wow, that was an understatement.

Not far away, in the same district of Maharashtra State, is a remarkable valley. In the seventeenth century, Mogul Emperor Aurangzeb moved the capital of his empire from Delhi to the Deccan Plateau in central India. Many Sufis went with him and headquartered themselves in a village called Khuldabad. Today, there are tombs of seven hundred saints and masters in this valley; it is called the Valley of the Saints. You can visit the tombs of genuine spiritual figures until you are intoxicated with the atmosphere. Rather than say your energies are recharged, speaking about the Valley of the Saints, you could say you feel blessed.

A Western city of immense blessedness is St. Francis's headquarters, Assisi, Italy. Francis was a fully God-realized master, a rare being to incarnate in the West. A trip to his tomb, San Damiano's, and his "little portion," the little chapel that served as Francis's headquarters, is one of the most sacred pilgrimages one can take in the West. Assisi was further sanctified when Meher Baba went into seclusion in a cave St. Francis used for his meditation and prayers. The cave is located near Carceri Monastery on Mount Sabasio. In 1932, Baba stayed in this cave for twenty-four hours. I visited the cave on three different occasions, and it remains one of my favorite places in the world, a true site of sacred pilgrimage.

Another sacred site associated with Meher Baba's universal work is in Switzerland. In 1934, Baba went into seclusion on a cliff-top near Schwyz called Fallenfluh. On this mountain, Baba had a meeting with the spiritual hierarchy, and the energy on this mountain still lingers after many decades. I've visited this sacred site twice.

A footnote to this discussion of sites related to saints and masters involves the appearance of supernatural beings. There are many such sites in the world, but I will only discuss one: the apparition of Our Lady of Guadalupe in Mexico. In December of 1531, the Virgin Mary manifested to a poor Indian peasant named Juan Diego. She appeared to him several times on a rocky hill north of Mexico City and performed at least three miracles. She healed his very sick uncle; she caused flowers to bloom on the rocky hilltop in midwinter; and finally, she manifested her image on a cloak Juan Diego was holding. This image of Our Lady of Guadalupe is revered by millions of Catholics, and the basilica where the image is displayed is the third most popular pilgrimage site in the world, attracting over ten million pilgrims each year.

If you want to be recharged, mentally, emotionally, physically, and spiritually, you can visit sacred sites around the globe. It's a magical way to unite the inner world with the outer, the subjective with the objective. And if you have a hard time feeling and experiencing spiritual energy and the vibrant currents of life or are in a psychologically low point of your life, I strongly recommend a spiritual pilgrimage. You might even be able to open yourself to the strongest current of energy: love. And love is the true bridge from the outer world to the inner divine planes.

CHAPTER 7

Reincarnation

Our next topic is one of my most favorites: reincarnation. You may wonder, "What does the philosophical idea of reincarnation have to do with unseen energies in everyday life?" Well, all experiences in life create sanskaras, or coded energy threads that are wrapped in bundles in the structure I termed the causal body. The causal body is a higher portion of the mind. Normally, the sanskaras are meted out in manageable configurations to create the subtle energetic backdrop of a particular lifetime.

However, the sanskaric threads from thousands and thousands of lifetimes are still there, coded in latent form, in our deepest unconscious mind. Many, many everyday experiences are tinted by this unconscious, yet personal, energy. And we get energy pulls and pushes, attractions and repulsions, sympathies and antipathies not only from surface sanskaras but also from echoes of sanskaric conditioning, perhaps from thousands of years ago. It's so common that I can guarantee you've been pushed or pulled by personal mental energy from ancient (and not-so-ancient) past lives. And again, I'll say that rather silly phrase: life can be a lot more fun and interesting when you're more aware of where these unseen energies and impulses come from.

Lord Buddha said that mind is "a bundle of thoughts." And all matter around us, on various levels, is nothing but consolidated mind. So layers and layers of mind are with us continuously. My teacher, Murshid MacKie, used to say that behind us is an army of past personalities, the mental sanskaras of countless past lives. Just imagine, in a way, we're at the head of our own personal army—so we must be the general.

I mentioned in an earlier chapter that the idea of reincarnation was the first door that opened for me internally and took me into the realms of spiritual interiority. It might be useful to give details of this awakening. In 1967, I was just eighteen and had joined the Theosophical Society. I had been out to dinner with a date, and we had closed the evening with a slightly chilly walk on a springtime beach of Lake Michigan. We debated the topic of reincarnation. We discussed atheism, the Christian concept of eternal heaven, after-death stories of spooks, and so on.

Somehow, in my thinking, I got to the point at some mental crossroad that either there was no life after death at all, or reincarnation had to be true. I looked up at the bright expanse of stars over the lake and yelled out to the universe, "If reincarnation is true, show me a sign." I don't even recall if the pleading was verbalized or not. All of a sudden, right where I was looking, a shooting star zoomed across the heavens. Then I looked to the right, and another meteorite appeared exactly where my gaze landed. Then I looked to the left, and a third streaked through the sky exactly where I was looking.

I said, "Okay, okay, okay, I got the message." I don't know if my lady friend saw the shooting stars. But for me, the answer to my cosmic question was given, and the riddle of life was solved.

Truly, if a human being is to reach perfection, "even as your father in heaven is perfect," reincarnation alone allows for that evolution of consciousness. Later that summer of 1967, I attended a theosophical lecture by Geoffrey Hodson, a seer from New Zealand. He made a remark that I remember clearly to this day: "Without reincarnation, life is a hopeless riddle."

But how does reincarnation work, and how are unseen energies involved? Every thought we have, every word we speak, and every action we do on earth creates an impression, a sanskara, a scratch on the mind, however you want to describe it. Each sanskara created is coded or conditioned by the energy of the initial action that created it. When the death of the physical body occurs, the coded sanskaras locked in the causal body remain. But they have been created through the energy of experiences on earth; therefore, they are connected to the gross plane of earth. Eventually, after some period of time, a bundle of these sanskaras seek expression; they want to expend their energy or, you might say, expand their energy by repeating the action that created them in the first place. It's kind of like when you have a habit, good or bad, you want to repeat that action. Sanskaras are like habits craving repetition.

This bundle of ego sanskaras, partially manifested in the subtle body, seeks a compatible vehicle for expression: a new body on earth. Although the new body will initially be created from the inherited sanskaras of the prospective mother and father, by age seven, the incarnating personality will have taken over and molded the body according to her or his own configuration or matrix of coded sanskaric fibers.

Every lifetime, therefore, your body is created, you might say, by energies of consciousness. The mind expresses itself in energy, and the energy creates forms on earth. But in addition to the "bundle of thoughts" that are released to create your current physical form, there are countless other sanskaras from countless other lifetimes lurking in latent form in the causal body. These also contain energy, and they can sometimes leak through the subtle membrane and create an echo of a memory of some long-past experience. Of course, in a general way, the newly created brain and etheric web block the recollections you might have of past lives. However, psychic leaks do occur.

Such leaks are most likely to occur during childhood, especially in the first seven years when the astral and etheric envelopes are loosely organized and more loosely connected to the physical body. I wrote about past-life memories in childhood in my book *The Secret Life of Kids.* In that work, I cite the research of the late, great Dr. Ian Stevenson of the University of Virginia, who studied children who had memories "suggestive of reincarnation." Here Dr. Stevenson discusses the evaluation of a typical case:

> A typical case of this type begins when a small child, usually between the ages of two and four, starts to tell his parents, and anyone who will listen, that he remembers living another life before his birth. ... A child claiming to remember a previous life usually asks to be taken to the place where he says he lived during that life. ... If the child has furnished enough details ... the search for the family he has been talking about is nearly always successful. ...

The child is then usually found to have been accurate in about ninety percent of the statements he has been making about the deceased person whose life he claims to remember. (Stevenson, *The Journal of Nervous and Mental Disease,* 1973, pp 307–308)

I've met many children who have occasional glimpses of past lives. Joshi, a four-year-old I met in Chicago, used to relive his death in his most recent life. He had been killed in a car crash. Every so often, Joshi would pretend to be steering a car. While "driving," he would talk to himself about the trip he was taking. Suddenly, an expression of horror and pain would come upon him. He would shield his face and twist his body and scream. "And then there was an accident and the car was all smashed up." Suddenly, he would completely relax, take a deep breath, and say out loud, "And then I was in the dead." As if remembering that others might be watching, he would look around, make contact, and cheerfully pat his own tummy and say, "And now Joshi is in here."

Memory signals from past lives can be confusing to children. When I was little, I used to feel I lived somewhere in brightly colored tents, with cozy cushions and patterned rugs inside. Since my cousin Ginny and I would build forts in her house with card tables and blankets, my child-mind thought my "tent home" must be in Ginny's house. I would wander all over her house, even in the attic and basement, looking for these tents. But I never could find my home. Of course, now it's clear to me that this Bedouin home in the desert was real. It was most certainly a memory coming through from a past life.

Even dreams can be a window into the past. A psychic once told me that if dreams are in color, they're more likely to stem from past-life experiences. Another child I knew, eleven-year-old John, had an epic three-night dream, which recurred every few months for several years. In the dream, he would be a boy in nineteenth-century Spain, who grew up by the sea and eventually became a clipper ship captain. On the third night of the dream, he would drown when his vessel sank. In waking life, John was obsessed with ships and constantly drew detailed clipper ships.

I think it is very interesting to have a look at your habits, character traits, books and movies you like, historical times that attract you, and places you like to travel to through the lens of possible past-life impressions. If you like to read Viking novels, doesn't it add a totally different dimension to be aware that you were most probably on that long ship sailing up the Norwegian fjord?

This hidden side of life helps make our daily experiences into deeply meaningful psychological connections and sometimes thrilling adventures. When Blake was growing up, I used to take him on three-week trips abroad each summer. It was very clear to both of us which countries felt like home and which did not. Our favorite trip was to Egypt, which must be an ancient homeland to practically everybody. Who didn't incarnate repeatedly in the deserts of Egypt? During many thousands of years, Egypt was simply the place to be.

But then there was Scotland. When Blake was eight, he stood in Glen Coe and said to me, "Dad, I've lived here before." Whenever we couldn't decide on a summer destination, Blake would say, "Let's go back to Scotland." It works the opposite way, too. One summer, we headed for Ireland. I always loved Irish music and dance, and I frequently told my schoolchildren Irish stories of the Little People. I fully expected to arrive at an ancient past-life homeland of mine. I didn't. Ireland was alien territory to me, and I did not feel at home there at all.

Sometimes, insights from past lives can explain present-day psychological issues and challenges. No doubt most phobias and obsessions originate in past lives. And have you ever met some stranger you just instantly "knew"? Surely such folks are past friends or relatives. During my first week in college, I went to a freshman mixer in my Berkeley dorm. I sat down across from this dark-haired fellow, and we just smiled at each other. This behavior was pretty strange to me because I was a very shy introvert. Anyhow, right then and there, he said his name was Bob and told me about Meher Baba, and I told him about theosophy. Bob and I have been best friends now for forty-seven years. We camped together, skied together, and we've traveled to India together five times. I think we must have been gypsy brothers in some past life.

Sometimes, past-life therapy can assist in untangling interpersonal issues. I don't generally advocate past-life hypnosis because I don't think putting your mind in a passive state, controlled by another, is a particularly smart idea. Such passive states can allow unpleasant astral forces or entities to have an effect on you. However, I know a close friend who was truly helped by a past-life vision that came to him through hypnosis.

Bill (I'll call him) had been happily married for fifteen years. Then his wife had an affair with an old high school sweetheart and asked Bill for a divorce. Bill insisted on trying couples therapy to save his marriage. In couples therapy, his wife said that she didn't trust Bill in their marriage. Bill was mystified: "She doesn't feel trust for *me*? She's the one who had the affair."

One day, Bill went to one of these psychic fairs, like a mini New Living Expo. He took a workshop with a hundred other people about gaining insights into life issues through past-life regression. Well, the three clients of this speaker-therapist did not show up. They were supposed to speak about how past-life revelations changed their lives. The speaker winged the presentation and said to the audience, "Why don't I just take all of you into a past life?"

Everyone was supposed to verbalize a current problem in life and follow along with the hypnotic visualization, repeating the question on this issue that needed clarification. Bill, of course, chose the question, "Why doesn't my wife trust me?"

The speaker led him in his mind to a grandfather clock. Bill opened the door of the grandfather clock, stepped behind the pendulum, and walked down a hallway. At the end of the hallway, he opened a door and stepped through. Then looked at his feet and his apparel, and then at his surroundings. He was quite surprised to find himself in riding attire—boots and pants—near a manor house that appeared to be in Victorian England. The story came into his mind in short visions of life scenes. Once he was in this past-life scenario, he simply knew what was going on.

Apparently, Bill was the son of a rich squire who had extensive lands tilled by indentured farmers. Bill was in love with the daughter of one of these peasant farmers, and he was planning on running away with her. This girl was none other than his current wife in his present life. When he told his father, the squire, of his plans, the squire said if he were to go through with his scheme, he would disown him and leave him penniless. Besides, Papa had already chosen a wife for his twenty-year-old son. Bill, instead of fighting for his love-relationship, simply gave in to his father, accepted the arranged marriage, and dumped the peasant girl.

When Bill came out of his vision and back to his present life consciousness, he knew that he had had a real glimpse into his most recent lifetime. Furthermore, he knew without a shadow of a doubt why his wife didn't trust him. And although his marriage was not saved, the past-life memory really helped Bill to reconcile himself with the difficult changes that come with divorce. You might say the glimpse into a past life was a transformative experience for him.

One favorite Meher Baba story illustrates another helpful side to understanding reincarnation. This was an incident that occurred with my first teacher, Murshida Ivy Duce, when she met with Baba in Myrtle Beach, South Carolina, in 1952. She was worried about her husband, Terry. I'll let Murshida continue:

> I was extremely tense for fear Terry would fail to reach the Center in time to meet Baba. He was down in Florida on a business trip. Baba, of course, easily discerned this and questioned on his board, "Are you still worried over Terry?" I assented. Baba raised his arm and traced a long back and forth swing in the air to illustrate what he was indicating on the board, "Ah, if you only knew how many husbands and wives you have had down through the ages, you would not worry so over this one!" (*How a Master Works,* p 90)

If a past-life memory can be so helpful in understanding present-life psychology, why can't we remember more past-life incidents? I've already mentioned how a fresh brain could not possibly register impressions of experiences it did not originally process. Plus, blockage of past-life memories is truly a divine mercy. Imagine if the experiences, travels, or people we knew all revealed hundreds of lifetimes' worth of memories. We would go crazy. What if we remembered how our spouse killed us in the sixteenth century or how she had been a child who had died at age seven of diphtheria in tenth-century Turkey? I'm quite sure such recollections would not help stabilize a current marriage. But that doesn't mean these lifetimes have no influence on us. The cumulative experiences and wisdom gained in the past form a powerful psychological backdrop to everything we experience now.

Meher Baba once told a Westerner, "When you begin a new lifetime on earth, you pick up where you left off last life. You always move forward, never backward."

Let's say you were a thief in a recent life and were hanged or put in prison. In this present life, if you were tempted to steal something, there would be a little voice deep within your mind, saying, "Don't do it." You simply would be blocked from stealing.

It sounds like the working of intuition. As a matter of fact, I've heard teachers say that exact thing: "The collective learning and wisdom gained from thousands of lifetimes of experience manifests as your intuition in this life." And if you've been a member of every race, ethnic group, and religion down through the ages, the mature, open, and spiritually minded person cannot be prejudiced against other races or religions, because they all belong to us, and we love them all.

Understanding reincarnation develops our compassion, sympathy, and love. We've been every type of person, lived in every type of environment, and experienced all the highs and lows of life. I know gentiles who encountered Jewish rituals and felt so moved, they converted to Judaism. My own godson met an Ethiopian girl and felt so at home in her culture, he bought them a home in Ethiopia and started a coffee plantation there. You join effortlessly with different ethnic groups or feel completely at home in foreign lands. It is reincarnation that unfolds magic and mystery in life and, at least for me, solves every existential riddle.

CHAPTER 8

Meditation

Individual, vital energy is a very personal thing. Some people have dependable energy for life in abundance. Some have very little. And still others have spurts of vitality, and then they have to regroup their etheric forces.

I am in this latter category, and I've always felt that this ebb and flow of vital, personal force had something to do with the fact that I have, in my astrological chart, five planets in the element of water. Water ebbs and flows. I have found over the years that the two most reliable ways to revitalize myself are short power naps and the practice of meditation.

For thousands of years, meditation has been an activity on the spiritual path. Recently, health practitioners tried to promote meditation as a tool not only for spiritual life but also for healthy living in general. It's a good a way to lower blood pressure, reduce stress, and so forth. But it's a rare person who can maintain a regular practice of meditation while completely divorcing it from the notion of spiritual progress. Virtually every spiritual system I'm aware of advocates some sort of daily meditation. And the various practices taught under the heading "meditation" are surprisingly varied and often unrelated to one another.

Spiritual progress, in my opinion, consists of gradually disintegrating the structures of the ego-personality, or unwinding sanskaras, and freeing and releasing these luminous fibers of mind from physical conditioning so they can connect to higher structures of mind on inner spheres. And in this process, psychic energy is released in the physical, emotional, and mental realms. Meditation can play a very helpful role in this process. And as the companion of Sri Aurobindo, referred to as the Mother, once said, "There are many forms of Energy. ... And it is through the various yogic exercises of breathing, meditation and concentration that one puts oneself in contact with these forms of Energy."

Although meditation practices are universal in helping to channel spiritual forces into one's physical body to help the material expression of the divine on earth, there are many, many different kinds of meditation. Some forms of meditation seem so different from one another, it's hard to imagine such varying practices all being called meditation.

Meher Baba once said, "There are as many paths to God as there are human souls." And there seems to be about as many types of meditation as well. Meditation practices no doubt vary according to the temperament of the seeker. In November 1967, as a freshman at the University of California in Berkeley, I had the opportunity to hear Maharishi Mahesh Yogi speak about meditation in the Berkeley Community Theater. I was initiated into mantra yoga shortly after hearing that talk and became active in the Student's International Meditation Society (SIMS) under Jerry Jarvis.

I took to meditation like a duck to water, and meditation changed my life. I remember early meditation sessions in which I felt like I was falling into a bottomless well. My inner being crackled with energy, and often I felt the pulse of inner currents for hours after a meditation session. In my first years of meditation, I would sometimes channel the rivers of life force, even when I wasn't meditating. Sometimes, the energy I released just seemed to swirl around me for an hour or so.

Baba said in his discourses that meditation is like a "picnic on the higher planes." For me, the meditative voyages into altered states of consciousness were dynamic and powerful. I felt I was tapping into vast stores of inner life force that I was able to use in daily life.

Maharishi claimed that meditation had the opposite effect on consciousness as LSD or marijuana. In fact, one must have been drug-free for two months to get a mantra from the SIMS group. One day, during spring break in my hometown of Wilmette, Illinois, Fred, a pal who liked drugs, encouraged me to smoke a little grass with him (I wrote about this incident in the chapter on drugs, but the story is important enough and interesting enough to tell twice). After I got high at Fred's house, I thought, *I'll test out Maharishi's assertion that meditation has the opposite effect of marijuana.* I started to meditate and amazingly was able to focus my attention on the mantra. After ten minutes or so, I noticed the tingling sensation of the cannabis was gone completely out of my bodily awareness. As I quietly sat on a chair, marveling at how I was simply straight again, suddenly the tingling feeling of the marijuana started climbing up my legs, up my torso, and finally reaching my head. I was completely stoned again. That was an impressive and unforgettable experiment in consciousness that proved to me that getting high from drugs was a very different quality of experience than the high that can come from deep meditation. And, I might add, that was the last time I ever used drugs.

Of course, not all of Maharishi's assertions were so reliable. I remember he promised "cosmic consciousness" after five years of meditation. And, if I recall correctly, "God consciousness" was promised after ten years. It's silly, in my opinion, to think you can meditate your way to God. The concept is that somehow, one opens an inner door to the mental world, and then the universal consciousness of the mental planes floods into awareness. Through meditation, you can catch a glimpse of the inner potential of your mind. But it doesn't last.

How could it? Our consciousness in daily life is locked on the experiences illuminated by our sanskaras. To lift the veil of our gross, down-to-earth experiences, we have to release the life energy locked in the coded sanskaric threads by balancing them out or by thinning them through interactions with people and things and events, and the resultant thoughts and feelings. We can fondly wish that advancing through inner, spiritual processes were as simple and easy as sitting in concentrated meditation.

But let's not underestimate the incredible value that glimpses of the inner light and higher realms can hold. Not only do such meditative experiences convince you of the truth of spiritual planes and refresh your weary days filled with the daily busy-ness of everyday life, but meditation can also inspire you to keep treading the spiritual path even in the face of calamity, doubts, misfortune, or setbacks, psychological or physical. Through meditation, these glimpses of the inner light and inner energies of the higher planes show the continual expansion of consciousness that awaits us all in the future.

For me, my daily meditation is the center of my life. It's like taking a swim in a clear, tropical spring. I look forward to it every day. And, after meditating for over forty-six years, I'd be lost without it. But I must confess to Maharishi that I still haven't found his cosmic consciousness, and it certainly is not for lack of trying.

But trying to fit meditation into your own personal, daily schedule seems like a logical and time-tested way to access prana or energy from the inner worlds. It also disciplines your mental powers and trains the monkey mind, these days distracted continually by ubiquitous digital devices, to concentrate.

How do you select a type of meditation to try? The first question to ask yourself is whether personal or impersonal meditation is appealing. Impersonal meditation has nothing to do with images of the divine or the teachings of spiritual figures. It usually consists of various techniques of training and focusing mental force, often through breathing exercises. In Buddhism, such practices are called Vipassana. An old friend of mine was an abbot of a Korean Zen center. The meditation he taught was simply to count your breaths. The meditator breathes in and out and thinks, *One.* The next inhalation and exhalation is *Two.* This goes on until the mind relaxes and becomes still (or until you forget where the count left off; in that case, you begin the breathing count again at one). It's really surprising at how peaceful, fresh, and clear you can become through such a simple practice.

Several years ago, a Taiwanese abbess taught another Buddhist meditation to my class of children when we visited the Buddha Gate Monastery during our school's World Religions Month. Her technique was to inwardly focus, with eyes closed, on the tip of the nose. She asked the children to be aware of the incoming and outgoing breath and the feeling of the air at the tip of the nose. These meditations are often termed mindfulness practices.

These two types attempt to rein in your scattered thoughts and bring the meditator to a state of thought-free awareness. There are many such impersonal types of meditation, many connected with Buddhist traditions. However, I think it may be hard for some Westerners to stick with such practices. I was recently reading Charles Tart's excellent book, *The End of Materialism.* In it, he quotes a Buddhist meditation teacher, Shinzen

Young, who says that in his classes, almost everybody becomes very enthusiastic about meditation. But, he notes, after about one year, only 5 percent are still meditators.

My own favorite meditation technique, however, is a more personal type that allows thoughts and feelings to be involved; it seems more enjoyable and fun. And people who try this technique tend to stick with it because it involves personal, mental interests and can be varied from day to day. But to me, it seems just as effective a way to quiet the mind and invite forceful inner energies and light into your being as any Vipassana practice.

In 1961, Eknath Easwaran from Kerala State in south India founded the Blue Mountain Center of Meditation in California. He developed a simple technique that came to be known as "passage meditation." In this practice, you silently repeat a passage from the writings of a spiritual figure or from a religious scripture. It's a type of "running meditation," as my first Sufi teacher, Murshida Duce, used to call it, in which the mind is free to think about ideas generated by the passage. But if the mind wanders, you return to the silent repetition of your chosen quote, prayer, or phrase, again and again.

I learned this technique because in 1967, the Blue Mountain Center of Meditation was around the corner from the cottage I rented as a university student. I used to go to the center several nights a week. Sri Easwaran would give a forty-five-minute talk each night about some religious tradition or mystical writer from the East or West, and then there would be a half-hour group meditation. Meditation with a group, I learned, is the easiest way to establish a regular practice, since the pranic energy generated by a room full of meditators kind of sweeps you along in a river of inner force. It's also a surefire way of demonstrating to a novice that there is definitely such a thing as inner, spiritual energy. Group meditation generates and focuses its palpable and powerful manifestation in an almost concrete way.

Of course, in those early university days, I was doing transcendental meditation. But passage meditation and TM are not unrelated. In the first, you mentally repeat a meaningful spiritual passage, while in the second, you silently repeat a mantra or sound, sometimes of unknown meaning. Someone who has mastered one technique can easily do the other. But again, I think passage meditation is more appealing, not only because you can choose a favorite, personal quote to use in meditation, but also you can change the memorized passage from day to day. Transcendental meditation, as in Buddhist mindfulness practices, can become boring because the meditator's heart is not involved.

Through the years, I've used my own spiritual master's name, Meher Baba, as well as meaningful passages from his books for my daily meditation practice. Another helpful aspect of Easwaran's passage meditation is that you can use a passage that is relevant to your day's experiences or mood. When I've had a really rough day and nothing seems to go right, I often meditate on this Baba quote: "The only real surrender is that in which poise is undisturbed through any adverse circumstance." Thus, meditation gives me a chance to celebrate another day, even if it's been a hard one.

Easwaran, incidentally, was the first person to teach a for-credit course on meditation at a major American university. His course in 1968 at UC Berkeley was attended by well over a hundred students. And I'll wager more than 5 percent of those students are still meditating today.

There are many helpful little ways to stimulate a good meditation, beyond having a simple, effective technique. It's helpful, for example, to have a specific place to meditate and to try to meditate at the same time each day. I have a little children's playhouse in my garden that I converted into a meditation room. I have been meditating in this room for more than forty years, and the baraka, or spiritual force, that's been built up in that room helps me go into a state of meditation merely by sitting down in there.

Many activities in life have certain supplies or accoutrements that go along with that activity. Just think of the helmet, outfit, and equipment a serious bicyclist uses. By putting on the bright, spandex uniform, bicyclists get in the mood to exercise. Or, an example near to my own life, when you put on a dramatic play with children, you don't just need your script; you also need props, backdrops, and cute costumes.

In meditation, the technique is the script. Now for the sets and props. If you're going to set up, say, a corner of your bedroom for your meditation area, you might begin by working on a little altar. It could have statues of spiritual figures, a crystal, a candle, and perhaps a bell. Bells and candles are nice because they generate their own special etheric energy, which aids in the meditation. Incense also activates its own force and can act to either calm the nerves of meditators or stimulate their thoughts or emotions. One author I studied suggested covering the altar in between practices with a diaphanous cloth. Unveiling the altar as you prepare for meditation can become a helpful and stimulating routine.

Finally, it can help to wear a costume. Draping a prayer shawl around your shoulders could be one way to tell your mind, "I'm just now entering the meditation zone." I put on a meditation mala, or necklace of special prayer beads. Almost all religions advocate the use of prayer beads or rosaries. If you use semiprecious stones, you're again introducing another type of etheric energy current into the process. I use tiger-eye beads, as they are said to stimulate meditative thinking.

Meditation can transform your life, and yes, it also has tremendous health benefits. It can help you unwind sanskaras and decondition your mind. It's also a skill that gives you something to do at those odd times when you're waiting for a train or stuck in an airport. It's a New Age alternative to surfing on your smart phone. It also can help you tune into nature. There's nothing more spectacular than meditating on the top of a mountain. When I visit sacred sites around the world, my first impulse is to sit down and meditate. I've done it in the Great Pyramid in Egypt, at Stonehenge, and at the base of California's Mount Shasta. Most recently, I meditated next to the Sacred Stone in Machu Picchu, Peru.

The impulse is quite natural because one wants to feel the unseen spiritual energies this book is describing. Meditation makes the life forces of the earth, the cosmos, and the interiority of the human being real, almost concrete. You can never subscribe to a materialistic philosophy if you have tasted the fruits of meditation. Try it. You could be in for an eye-opening spiritual treat.

CHAPTER 9

Drugs

In a book written about how energies in the unseen realms affect our daily lives in physical bodies, it may seem surprising to find a chapter on drugs. Sacred sites, the mineral kingdom, astrology: sure. But how does the topic of drugs fit in?

For thousands of years, drugs and herbs of various kinds have been a part of vision quests, spiritual awakenings, and shamanic initiations. They are certainly something one comes across while reviewing spiritual literature. I was recently in Machu Picchu and bought a book on the spiritual awakening of a young Russian seeker. I was surprised to find his whole spiritual quest was centered on drugs. In the 1960s and early 1970s, especially in America, psychedelic and hallucinogenic drugs were touted as the quick road to heaven, the easy way to open up to visions and energies of the inner worlds.

However, in my humble opinion, various drugs, particularly LSD and marijuana, can open you to negative energies from the lower astral plane; entities want a whiff of that drug aroma, and some drugs even can cause serious damage and rips in the etheric web, which is the superphysical mechanism that transmits higher mental and emotional forces to our brain, nervous system, and endocrine system.

As with all sections of this book, I'm going to share my own experiences and knowledge, and not try to prove every statement by pinning it to authoritative spiritual or scientific research. I certainly know very little, for example, about the chemistry of drugs or the long-term effects of recreational drug use. However, despite my lack of a certain type of expertise, I think it's very important for spiritual students to examine the occult side of getting high.

In 1966, Meher Baba said, "The most important service to the world at present is to make people stop taking drugs." Quite an impressive and sweeping statement. It came in response to questions Baba had been asked by young people experimenting with various drugs, largely in America. Three young men at Harvard wrote questions for Baba to answer in his headquarters in India. These three friends were Richard Alpert, Allan Cohen, and Tim Leary.

Baba replied that "mind-changing" drugs, specifically LSD, mescaline, psilocybin, and marijuana, were harmful physically, mentally, and spiritually and should never be taken by spiritual aspirants. It's interesting to note that Baba always included marijuana in his list of harmful drugs, especially in the light of people nowadays going on campaigns to legalize pot and label it "less harmful than alcohol."

When I was initiated as a mureed (or student) of Meher Baba's Sufism Reoriented, one of my vows to Murshida Ivy Duce was to never take hallucinogenic or psychedelic drugs, including marijuana. Apparently, when you are stoned on grass, vibrations generated by the brain, and broadcast subtly through the etheric aura, are of a particularly slow and dense quality. This dense radiated field attracts unpleasant astral entities and passing thought forms that vibrate in sympathy to this gross energy. Unpleasant energies are amplified, and psychic trouble can arise.

My first introduction to this problematic nature of marijuana did not come through Meher Baba, but rather through Maharishi Mahesh Yogi. As a young theosophist and freshman at UC Berkeley in 1967, I went to a lecture by Maharishi, introducing his transcendental meditation. He said that the energies of drug use have the opposite effect as the psychic energies generated from meditation. The two practices were in such opposition that he would not allow people to be initiated into transcendental meditation unless they had been drug-free for two months.

Fortunately, I had only experimented with pot a few times during the previous summer. Although I certainly enjoyed the high, I wasn't terribly interested in repeating the experience, even though drugs of all kinds were readily available to university students in Berkeley. So when I was initiated into TM, my recreational drug use was over … almost.

During my college years, I would fly home to Illinois for Christmas and spring vacations. During spring break of 1968, I was hanging out with one of my best high school buddies. Whereas I had learned to get high by meditation, my friend had expanded his drug use at Columbia University. "Sex and drugs and rock 'n' roll" truly became his college motto. Anyhow, he invited me to smoke marijuana with him. I accepted. I don't know quite what possessed me, because by this time, I was also acquainted with Baba, who had a negative view on drug use. But I did it anyway. I got stoned, very stoned. Somehow in the cloud of my altered brain, I recalled that Maharishi said meditation was the opposite of pot use. It took consciousness "up," whereas pot smoking took consciousness "down." I decided to try to do transcendental meditation, even though I was stoned.

Surprisingly, I was able to concentrate on my mantra, enough to ascend to a pretty good meditative state. As I've written elsewhere, I took very easily to meditation and was quite good at it. After around ten minutes, I opened my eyes and discovered I was completely straight. I wasn't at all high anymore. The effects of the marijuana were completely gone. And I had only gotten high half an hour ago. The effects should have been at their peak.

Wow. Whatever effects the marijuana had on my brain and nervous system, the meditation seemed to cancel out. Meditation really was the opposite of getting high. This was a tremendously exciting realization for me. No wonder Baba and Maharishi told people to stop taking drugs. If people long for spiritual growth and the experience of spiritual planes, they can't take drugs. Drugs take consciousness in the opposite direction. Meditation takes you into spiritual dimensions. Marijuana takes you deeper into the dense, material dimensions. No wonder the physical senses seem to get more acute, especially the sense of taste.

While I was marveling at my little psychic experiment, all of a sudden, the buzzing and tingling started in my feet and slithered up my body like a snake. The feeling of the marijuana high ascended through my heart to my brain, and I was completely 100 percent stoned again. And I stayed stoned throughout the rest of the evening.

But the lesson had been learned. March 1968 was the last time I ever smoked weed. I was in good shape for what awaited me. The next year, I went to India for Meher Baba's last darshan, and the year after that, I was initiated as a Sufi. Murshida Duce required one year of being drug free before she accepted someone as her student.

When I had my interview to become part of her Sufi school, she asked me if I had ever taken LSD. I said no. She replied, "You don't know how lucky you are."

Another of Murshida Duce's instructions to her students involved being in social situations where drugs were being used. She said that if we ever found ourselves at a party or gathering of friends where marijuana was being smoked, we should politely excuse ourselves and get away from there as quickly as possible. The drug vibrations apparently can attract unpleasant astral thought forms or spooks that can attach themselves to your aura and accompany you home.

Dr. Allan Cohen told me a very interesting story that involved Frances Sakoian, a dear friend of his. Frances was a well-known astrologer in the Boston area and the author of nineteen books on the subject. She was, over the years, the president of the New England Astrological Association, a producer of a television program on astrology, and the first to offer a fully accredited university course on astrology in the United States.

Anyhow, in the early 1960s, Allan had met and befriended Frances. She became a dear auntie to him. Frances, in addition to being an excellent astrologer, was also clairvoyant and a psychometrist (which will be discussed later).

In 1964, Dr. Tim Leary had acquired a sprawling mansion in upstate New York called the Millbrook Estate. This became his laboratory retreat for experimenting with hallucinogenic drugs. At the time, Allan Cohen and his two mentors, Alpert and Leary, had already heard from Meher Baba about the dangers of drug use. But Dr. Leary was not about to give up his drug trips. He was still convinced that LSD could open one up to genuine spiritual experiences. In fact, I saw him at the Whole Life Expo in 2000 in San Francisco, and he still was convinced you could find "God in a pill."

Well, Allan decided to invite his friend Frances Sakoian to Millbrook to see what her clairvoyance might reveal. In the scheme I use of twelve senses, clairvoyance is the tenth sense, the ability to perceive the astral world through an extension of the sense of sight. Clairvoyance is "clear seeing." Frances was horrified to see a giant astral octopus-like creature surrounding the entire Millbrook house. It had red and black tentacles slithering into every room, searching out sources of human vitality to absorb. Drugs expand and destabilize the etheric body and make the human life force vulnerable to outside entities. This psychic octopus was a true vampire, sucking etheric force from the people Dr. Leary had invited to Millbrook for guided LSD trips.

There was one young man there, a familiar fellow to Allan, who slept all the time. He would sleep for at least sixteen hours a day. Frances could see why: He had a tentacle of the astral apparition wrapped around his body several times, leeching his vital force. He literally didn't have the energy to stay awake.

Allan said to me, incidentally, that Dr. Leary also caught glimpses of this psychic octopus on more than one occasion. He ignored the visions, however, choosing to believe they were just passing LSD hallucinations.

Another story involving Frances was that she was once speaking to a large group of college students on astrology when she interrupted herself to give an aside: "You know, I can clearly see," she said, "which one of you smoke marijuana. It's visible to me in your aura as a brown smudge over the liver. The liver has to do the work of cleansing the THC from your body. It takes two years for the liver to rid the body of the toxic effects of marijuana."

Another interesting experience I had occurred when I joined the Theosophical Society in early 1967. In July 1967, I attended my first convention and summer school of the American Section at Olcott, the headquarters in Illinois. A renowned clairvoyant was the featured speaker. He was an elderly man from New Zealand named Geoffrey Hodson. One of the topics for the morning lecture was "The Psychedelic and Yogic Pathways to Reality." In this talk, Hodson spoke about how practicing Raja yoga could transform you spiritually and open you up to inner dimensions. This activated, yogic energy would possibly open up chakras and influence other states of consciousness. He said it could also come through experimentations with LSD and marijuana. The dangers here were that drugs would blast open an inner doorway without being under any control of the aspirant. The basic point was that drugs and meditation lead to the same goal, only drugs were a more haphazard and dangerous route.

The following fall, Hodson's itinerary took him to the Theosophical School of Wisdom at the Krotona Institute in Ojai, California, where he was going to repeat his talk from Olcott. However, an eye-opening experience awaited him in California. Many young people from the Los Angeles area showed up for his lecture. As a trained clairvoyant, their drug-abused auras were plainly visible to him. Rather than any spiritual openings, he saw for the first time the true effects of using LSD and marijuana. He saw that the etheric brains of the drug users "looked like oatmeal," and that the effect of drugs, rather than leading to the clarity of meditative thinking, actually resulted in damaged auras and confused and muddled minds.

In the revised lecture, in word and published form, Hodson retracted his earlier theory about drugs. Now he urged people to take up the meditative path to spiritual reality and to shun drugs, which injure the fine nervous tissue of the physical body and actually damage the etheric counterpart of the brain.

A close friend of mine, Robbie Basho, a famous guitarist in the 1970s and 1980s, attested to the permanent psychic harm drugs can do. He told me that his experiments with drugs produced a rip in his etheric membrane that left him vulnerable to all kinds of horrible astral energies for the rest of his life. The etheric rip also opened up a degree of clairvoyance that wasn't helpful for him, either.

The etheric web is the occult mechanism for transferring superphysical impressions and energies from the higher anatomy into the nervous and endocrine systems of the physical body. Without this bridge of consciousness, the etheric body, the inner person, could not communicate with the outer person. In fact, the vital body of the etheric realm is the giver of life. When it leaves the body, you die. In addition, the etheric body acts as a shield, blocking conscious perception of unseen energies. Without this etheric shield, we would be continually bombarded with all sorts of inner stimuli: thought forms, memories of past lives, vibrations, and energies emanating from virtually all things living, nonliving, and dead. It might sound like a most interesting experience to lose the protection of this web, but the overflow of psychic information would drive you crazy.

Robbie Basho suffered continually because his web leaked. In addition to severe sleep issues, Robbie could not be in any environment where drugs were being used. The muddy, gray-brown energies in the astral world, summoned by drug use, would cause him physical pain. Pain was his constant companion, mainly attacking the centers along his spine. I often drove him to doctors whom he hoped would alleviate his suffering. And Robbie's clairvoyance did not help matters, either. Of course, at our Sufi classes, he was able to perceive the golden light coming from our teacher. But when he went home to Berkeley, he saw many unpleasant things. The etheric leak in his damaged bridge mechanism allowed him glimpses of the lower astral levels. He could see if someone was stoned because his etheric body would be a muddy gray, expanded, vague, and sometimes jagged around the edges, and the person would radiate a distinctly unpleasant energy. Also, of course, Robbie saw plenty of spooks and astral imps, nasty things with distinctly low vibes. Robbie could have been a poster boy for the campaign "Just say no to drugs."

In 1971, another spiritual teacher was alerting her students to the dangers of drug use. The Mother, the spiritual companion of South India's Sri Aurobindo Ghose, inaugurated a unique city of light she called Auroville. She promised to set down no rules of living for the international citizens of Auroville. However, in March 1971, an Aurovillian sought an interview with her:

> You said you did not want to make rules for Auroville. But recently you wrote, "Drugs (particularly Ganja) are forbidden in Auroville." Have you changed your view of Auroville?" The Mother replied, "Perhaps Aurovillians have not yet attained the level of consciousness expected of them." (*The Mother's Agenda*, vol. 12, p 62)

In the early 1970s, Allan Cohen's friend Frances Sakoian was invited out to California in her capacity as a master astrologer. Allan was friends with a lab technician who worked for the Drug Enforcement Administration in Berkeley. He casually mentioned to his friend that Frances would be in town and it might be interesting to have her psychometrize various drugs.

According to a scheme that differentiates the various types of psychic experiences, people have twelve senses. The first five are the familiar physical senses, and the remaining seven are the so-called psychic senses. Everyone has these extra senses in the astral realm. But for most of us, the etheric web blocks them from coming through to physical awareness. Frances, as we've already seen in Millbrook, had the tenth sense, or clairvoyance. She also possessed the eleventh sense, often referred to as psychometry: the ability to pick up information from an object or person by an extension to the sense of touch. A psychometrist can read the sanskaras that make up an object.

It's interesting to note that spiritually minded people often avoid antiques. The reason is that every object holds the sanskaras of the maker of the object, the various owners, and the environments where the object has been. Let's say an antique vase has been on display in a corner of a fancy restaurant. Psychometrists, just holding the vase, could tune into (maybe even visually) the sanskaras of the potter in China who fashioned the vase. They could also detect the various owners down through the decades and even sense the energies of the maid who dusts it, or the patrons of the restaurant who admire it. Sanskaras hold coded energies and are part of the physical matrix of everything on earth.

The possibility of Frances tuning into various drugs in the DEA laboratory intrigued the lab technician. The technician opened the DEA office on Sunday for Allan and Frances, since such psychic experimentation would probably be best to keep secret. He had previously prepared several opaque, brown-colored vials. Each vial had a different drug. Frances was supposed to hold each one in her hands and describe what the drug was like and what effects it had.

I was told the results of her experiments when I got back to the university in the fall. And, as a matter of fact, I used her research as significant points in the antidrug talks I gave at schools. I was a member of the Committee for Psychedelic Drug Information, and our group gave presentations at junior high and high schools.

As she held the first vial, Frances reported that this was a very powerful drug, but that it could have great social benefits. It was birth-control pills. The second opaque vial she psychometrized she called an even more powerful drug. It should never be taken recreationally, but that under the supervision of a trained psychologist, the drug could have some use in a therapeutic setting. It was LSD.

As she was reaching for the third vial, she suddenly pushed it away with the back of her hand. She said the vibrations of the energy from that bottle were so low and gross and unpleasant, she didn't even want to touch it with her hand. That vial was filled with marijuana.

The fourth vial was a little test included by the lab tech. It was a rare Chinese drug called Yen-Chi. It was "twice-cooked" opium brought home from the war in Vietnam. Frances held the vial, closed her eyes, and started sobbing. Allan asked her what was wrong. She said a deceased man on the astral plane came to her and told her he tried to help drug addicts who died. Apparently, it's very difficult after death to slough off a lifetime of drug addiction. It's a version of an after-death state that psychologically could be called hell. The gentleman said people on earth have to know the dangers of addiction and know how horrible it is to die while still addicted.

Meher Baba said that psychoactive drugs such as LSD and marijuana are harmful physically, mentally, and spiritually. He said that the physical and subtle bodies can be so imbalanced and damaged by drug use that all spiritual progress can sometimes be rendered impossible for an entire incarnation.

Clairvoyants who describe what they see when they observe someone stoned or on an LSD trip often observe an aura that has a blurry haze over it. This haze indicates that there is a lack of articulation between the etheric sheath and the physical nervous system. Over time, the lack of interface with inner mental and emotional energies and the physical body causes chronic exhaustion and tremendous loss of mental clarity. I remember talking on the phone one time to someone who had been smoking pot daily for several years. In the course of the twenty-minute conversation, he repeated the same stories. It was really almost like speaking to someone with dementia.

A Chinese doctor in Maui, Hawaii, was trying to build up the chi of a patient through weekly acupuncture treatments. He wasn't having good results. Finally, he discovered the patient was a daily marijuana smoker. The doctor informed the patient he would not work on him anymore unless he gave up marijuana use. The marijuana was disrupting the energies he was trying to build up through his acupuncture.

In summary, from the spiritual point of view, psychedelic drug use is not nearly as benign as folks in the "legalize marijuana" movement claim. It can cause rips and imbalances in the subtle bodies. It gives off a very low, gross vibration that can attract low thought forms and unpleasant astral entities. Anyone who really understands the hidden side of drug use most assuredly will "just say no."

CHAPTER 10

The Mineral Kingdom

In David Spangler's excellent book *Subtle Worlds*, he says, "It helps to practice paying attention to subtle energies, such as those in the room or around objects, and developing your 'energy senses'" (p 186).

For the last thirty-five years or so, I have been attracted by the energies of the mineral kingdom and tried to become sensitive to minerals, crystals, and gemstones. In a fascinating description in Spangler's book, he discusses an arc of the astral plane, which is one "of stone and mineral, a world devoid of organic life, but vibrant with the living energies within minerals" (p 137). Imagine a world of gigantic crystals and mineral shapes, a forest of giant crystal points. This is a place I'd like to visit.

Why are crystals and gemstones associated with New Age thinking, healing, and energy work? And why are spiritual students attracted to the mineral kingdom? Crystals, minerals, and gemstones focus spiritual forces and radiate etheric energy. Of course, everything in creation radiates etheric force. But why is the force of crystals special? It has something to do with the color, shape, and composition of crystals. The best analogy I can think of is the prism. A clear piece of glass, shaped in a particular way, has the ability to focus a ray of sunlight and transform it into a ray of colors. In a similar way, the color, shape, and clarity of a crystal focuses and radiates etheric energy.

An example of how shape alone can affect the flow of energy comes from pyramidology: the very shape of the Great Pyramid focuses and radiates spiritual energy. At one point in my teaching career, I made a large cardboard pyramid and placed it on a stand. I put pillows under it, and it became a Reading Temple. Several clairvoyant children saw blue, etheric spheres of light rising from the apex of the pyramid. And inside the Reading Temple, they saw a brilliant beam of light, almost like a laser, shining down from the apex and going right through the floor. The point of a crystal in some ways resembles the shape of a pyramid. So the shape of an object on the earth plane can affect the energy it holds. Crystals also come from the earth and can help human beings feel connected to Mother Earth.

Let's see what Melody, in the book *Love Is in the Earth,* can contribute to this discussion:

> Crystals have been used and/or revered since the dawn of civilization. The Christian *Bible* refers to crystals over two hundred times. The energies of the mineral kingdom are "universal energies." Hence, when one contacts and is willing to receive this energy, and begins to exercise personal creativity via exercise of the Higher Will, one can contact and synthesize the energies from which the entire universe is comprised.
>
> This is the reason that crystals and other minerals are so very powerful. ... Use of the mineral kingdom further stimulates the melding of one's personal energy with that of the mineral kingdom. (pp 31–32)

As a good New Age spiritual student, I've always enjoyed crystal stores and crystal displays at New Age expos. Somehow, crystals have become a part of the contemporary spiritual scene. But it was only gradually that I started to appreciate the subtle radiance of gems and crystals, rather than merely enjoying their extraordinary beauty.

In 1979, as I approached my marriage, my fiancée and I wanted to create spiritually charged rings. We wanted to select just the right gemstones for both our wedding rings.

With five planets in water signs, you would think I would most appreciate emotions and the feeling nature of life. But I found the way for me to open up to my feelings is through understanding, through the intellect. So in 1979, I started studying metaphysical books on gems and minerals to see if I could discover what gem should adorn our wedding rings.

In a pamphlet by Edgar Cayce, I found a section that touted lavender jade as an especially good, healing stone for Pisces. My wife and I were both Pisces, so we selected lavender jade for both our wedding rings.

The examination of gems and crystals then found a permanent place in my metaphysical studies. When I divorced, I replaced the lavender jade with the Star Ruby I had purchased in Chennai, India. Wearing a ruby was said to help in developing an individual, independent life. That's exactly what I needed at that time in my life. Rings later became a sort of trademark for me. Men can wear gems on rings, and it doesn't seem weird (or at least not too weird). Now I wear two rings on each hand. My right-hand pinky ring changes day by day. If I feel somewhat ill, I'll put on my emerald ring, which stimulates physical health. If I'm feeling emotionally low, I'll put on my amber ring, which counteracts depression.

Gemstone rings not only carry the specific energy of the jewels, they can also be magnetically charged by human beings. If a person wears a gemstone ring every day, the ring will be magnetized with etheric force, either pleasant or unpleasant, depending on the temperament of the owner. In a word, rings can hold blessings or curses.

History, literature, and folklore are ripe with stories of magic rings and power crystals. Just read Tolkien. One has a dragon guarding jewels under a mountain, while hobbits, Bilbo and Frodo, search for a magic ring, a ring of power. Such archetypal concepts hold a great deal of truth.

A friend of mine once picked up a nice gemstone ring from an estate sale and proudly wore the rather large ring on the ring finger of her right hand. I don't recall now what the stone was that was set in the gold ring. Anyhow, she started having ill health, and various accidents occurred to her. After some time, her mother suggested she consult Irene, a rather good psychic they knew. Irene said it was the ring. The ring had been worn by a very depressed lady who later committed suicide. The ring was cursed with the sanskaras of its previous owner. It was so unlucky that my friend was told not to risk another person wearing it. "Throw it into the middle of a body of water," Irene suggested. So my friend threw the ring into the middle of a nearby lake. Her health immediately improved.

A bishop in the Catholic church must wear an amethyst ring. This is no silly superstition. Amethyst is the regal stone, said to support transformative spirituality, stimulating the heart and throat chakras: all in all, a perfect stone for a bishop.

These are just a couple examples of how rings can hold powerful energies and how stones can be charged with the force of the owner.

But my gemstone fun does not stop with rings on my fingers. Pocket stones can be even larger than ring gems. Greeks are known for their "worry beads," little plastic beads they keep in their pockets and fiddle with when they're sick or nervous. My worry beads are pocket stones: a gem or crystal that fits in my pocket. The specific etheric energy of each stone dictates which one I will pop in my pocket each day. As David Spangler suggests, over the years, I have developed my "energy senses." I'll take out my collection of stones and scan them, sometimes even with my hand, to select the day's stone. Sometimes, I'll wake up and just know I need lapis lazuli in my pocket that day. It's fun to become truly knowledgeable about and friendly with minerals. Some become close energy friends and some even best friends, while many others just remain acquaintances.

I have an ongoing discussion with an agnostic friend about how understanding the hidden side of life makes living more interesting and more fun. Feeling the earth energies of crystals might well be partly in your imagination. However, a Jungian professor, Dr. Stephan Hoeller, recently told me that imagination is precisely the key in beginning to feel the energies of unseen realms. And the joy of feeling that everything in creation is alive, and we actually can attune ourselves to the energies of minerals, plants, and animals, does indeed make life more meaningful. Imagination isn't a problem; it's a transcendental tool.

My late teacher, Murshid MacKie, said that the energies from stones and crystals were more pronounced in earlier epochs, as was human receptivity to their power. But the forces are still very much present, and he himself, from time to time, would need a certain gemstone for his spiritual work. Speaking of spiritual work and crystals, Meher Baba's headquarters were literally built on hills of quartz crystals. And the hill behind his house is so littered with crystals, they're just lying on the pathway to the top.

One of Baba's masters, the great Sadguru Narayan Maharaj of Kedgaon, India (1885–1945), had as one of his jobs to work with the mineral kingdom. His seclusion or meditation room was underground. He also wore gems. Several of his coats had diamond buttons, and he frequently wore gold and precious stones as rings, bracelets, and necklaces. He also sat on a silver throne.

To reach his underground chamber, one opened a concealed door and had to bow down to descend a tiny, narrow staircase. On three occasions, I've sat quietly in that room, and the baraka, or spiritual force, is astonishing.

One amazing experience my wife and I had recently was a visit to the Crystal Room, a store in Mount Shasta City, California. It's kind of a crystal lover's dream come true: room after room filled with crystal displays. One room was sort of a meditation room with chairs and soft music playing. Around the walls of the room were six gigantic crystal points, on bases that were illuminated in such a way that the crystals were filled with golden light. The points range from two to four feet high. Two of them were citrine, and the rest were clear quartz. If you want to feel the spiritual, electrifying charge of the mineral kingdom, this is the room to visit. Hana and I were stunned to feel the tingling energy of that room all over our bodies. It was almost like entering a new dimension. We practically staggered to chairs, closed our eyes, and were zapped with the amazing power of the crystals. We were swept into an instant meditative state.

Another way of surrounding yourself with crystal energy is through wearing spherical beads around your neck. Michael Katz, the author of *Gemstone Energy Medicine*, and his wife, Ginny came in touch with beings from the spiritual world who worked with the energies of minerals. Their psychic contact with these "Gemstone Guardians" opened up for them, and their readers, the field of gemstone therapy. These guardians suggested that the energies of crystals can best be absorbed by human beings if the gemstones are fashioned into a spherical shape. Thus, beads worn around the neck can allow the energy to permeate your aura. A necklace of such beads touches the back of the throat chakra and hangs down right over the heart chakra. Depending on the nature, clarity, and size of the precious and semiprecious stones, wearing gemstone beads can have certain emotional and mental effects. They even can be used to treat and heal various physical health conditions. Katz in *Gemstone Energy Medicine* delineates the nature of energy emitted by various gemstones and how wearing beads can help heal various conditions.

Discovering this information was a dream come true for me. Now I use the mineral energy more consciously and more effectively; I carry stones around with me whenever I want to.

When I was teaching school, I would diagnose how I was feeling after a long day with my students, and then when I went home, I would treat my condition with a necklace of semiprecious stones. For instance, if I felt emotionally drained, I would wear mother of pearl beads. If I felt stressed out from a difficult parent conference, I would use howlite beads. If I felt depressed, amber would come to the rescue. If I felt I was coming down with a cold, I would immediately don my bloodstone necklace or dark green aventurine (ideally, I would have had an emerald necklace, but such precious gemstones are not in the budget of a schoolteacher). When I didn't know what stone to wear, I put on a strand of lapis lazuli. Edgar Cayce said that lapis lazuli was the best overall mineral for people to use. It helps with almost all conditions of the mind and body.

Eventually, I discovered the value of beads in my spiritual life. I purchased my first beads in India in 1987. I was walking on Juhu Beach just north of Bombay when I met a fifteen-year-old boy selling necklaces. I bought a strand of tigereye beads. Later, I placed the strand on an altar in a place of pilgrimage, thinking to charge them with extra spiritual life force. For the next thirty-two years, I would wear these beads every day in my meditation session. In researching tigereye in various manuals about using crystals, the mineral tigereye was always mentioned as an aid to meditation.

One of my Sufi preceptors mentioned using prayer beads to repeat my mantra. Using the hands can be an effective way to focus the mind. Maria Montessori always said in childhood, the hands are hardwired to the brain. So I immediately found that using beads while repeating my mantra was fun and helped me concentrate. I started restringing my necklaces with heavy-duty fishing line and leaving a space on the necklace so that the beads could be moved slightly by my fingers. Thus, my gemstone necklaces became my prayer beads.

Almost every world religion has a tradition of using prayer beads: Christianity, Hinduism, Buddhism, Islam, Sikhism, and even Zoroastrianism. There's an ancient story about Zoroaster throwing his prayer beads at his murderer. In Buddhism and Hinduism, the mala (or beads) are usually made of sandalwood or some other wood. Of course, in Christianity, the rosary is made of glass beads. But in every sacred tradition, a bead necklace is always used as a tool for helping to concentrate when praying, meditating, or remembering the name of God. Muslims have the most practiced use of prayer beads. In the Hadiths, there is a story of Mohammed's daughter, Fatima, asking her dad, "How can I feel closer to God?" Mohammed replied that she should use prayer beads and with each bead say three prayers: "Subhan Allah," "Al-hamdu," and "Allahu Akbar." There are ninety-nine beads on a Muslim strand. They are called Fatima beads, or *misbaha*. These beads can be made of many things, but I've been told the best beads are made out of stone. Muslims never wear them around the neck, but rather they are carried in your pocket.

Using gemstone beads just gives another little energy boost to your spiritual practices. In my scheme of seven psychic senses, the tenth sense includes the ability to know the properties and uses of minerals and crystals. But as David Spangler mentioned at the beginning of this chapter, people can develop their "energy senses" to tune in to the forces radiated through crystals and gems. It's another way to make the hidden side of life part of your everyday awareness.

I'd like to close this chapter with a story about one of my favorite spiritual figures, Jiddu Krishnamurti. Krishnaji's secretary and attendant and best friend for the last twenty-five years of his life was a lady named Mary Zimbalist. Mary would travel the world with her famous companion, but when he journeyed to India, which she didn't much care for, she would go back to Ojai, California, by herself. Krishnamurti would worry about her, and one of the ways he sought to protect her was through use of the mineral kingdom. Mary had a special family ring she wore, with three precious gemstones. Before K would leave her, he'd ask for her ring. Sometimes, he would wear it himself for a day and a night, and other times, he would just put the ring on his bedside table overnight. Then he would give it back to her, saying, "Now this ring will protect you." Mary always noticed that after K had the ring, the gold and the jewels would sparkle brightly, as if they had just been polished by a jeweler (Scott Forbes, *Krishnamurti: Preparing to Leave*, 2018).

Everything in creation is alive with force. And it's a delight to be able to share in the specific energy from the mineral kingdom.

CHAPTER 11

Gardening

In the book *The Elves of Lily Hill Farm,* nature spirits advise the author, Penny Kelly, in agricultural practices. One elf gave her this advice: "The basis of yer reality is the world of nature. We all come from the world of nature. Lose that direct connection and ye will lose the whole reality because ye've lost your base." Whether you live in a small apartment or a grand estate, the method of keeping a daily connection with nature alive is through gardening. Becoming the conscious custodian of a small corner of Mother Earth through the creation of a garden is nurturing on psychological and spiritual levels. Not only is the garden a venue for happy work outdoors, but an established garden acts as a sanctuary where you can retreat to recharge your energy after a hectic day in the modern, stress-filled world.

I call a garden "civilized nature." Rather than just observing and being refreshed by nature in Yosemite or the Grand Canyon, a garden is intimate, where there's a give and take between yourself and the plants and flowers and stones. The garden nourishes you, and you, in turn, nurse the garden.

Connecting with nature surely has an important place in the life of the spiritual student. The great spiritual teacher, Jiddu Krishnamurti, once said, "The mind loses its sensitivity whenever there is no communication with nature. Live close to nature." Meher Baba, looking out from a mountaintop in Ojai, California, said, "Now go out and see the view and try to love [God] through nature" (*Lord Meher*, p 4067). Gardening is a way to bring nature into your own home and your own daily life.

The theme of this book is recognizing and collaborating with energies from the unseen realms. Gardening introduces us to one of the sweetest ways we can collaborate with these forces. The plant kingdom shares with human beings the inner energy matrix we refer to as the etheric field or the subtle physical body. It is through this matrix that plants, animals, and humans absorb energy from food, the sun and earth, and other forces in the environment. Spending time around plants, and especially trees, can sensitize you to the types of occult currents used for plant growth.

I remember a statement by the theosophical seer, C. W. Leadbeater. He said that if you are feeling low or depleted energy, you can lie on the earth with your head facing north, near a pine tree or a eucalyptus tree. To rest in that position for fifteen minutes will replenish the supply of the etheric life force. Why? Well, pine trees and eucalyptus trees radiate more prana, more life force than any other member of the vegetable kingdom. Lying near this radiation infuses us with this helpful energy. I planted a eucalyptus tree in my own garden to experiment with this type of prana. I didn't realize, however, that the Australians call this tree a gum tree for a reason. Gooey resin continually sweats out of the tree, making a restful lie-down near it almost impossible. I still love my eucalyptus tree, however, and one way I can appreciate the strong energy it holds is to observe its amazingly fast growth.

One footnote to this discussion of life force: An interesting metaphysical explanation I've heard against raising and eating genetically modified foods (GMFs) is that the modification process robs the plant of much of its etheric energy. GMF plants simply do not have the same life force, whether in the ground or on the dinner table.

But let's return for a moment to the subject of trees. After all, trees certainly became an important part of any garden. In the immediate years after I started my daily meditation practice, I became quite sensitive to the power of trees, particularly large deciduous trees: elms, oaks, maples, and so on. I was raised in the North Shore of Chicagoland. I remember Lake Street, for instance, was lined with towering elm and oak trees. The lofty branches would make a huge archway for a mile or so down the street. I would experiment and slowly approach one of these giants. At what point would I start to feel the tree's force, its aura? I would love to soak up this glow and would often stand with my back against the tree; at other times,

I would hug the tree, partly to share its energy and partly to thank this being for its role in my life and in all life on earth. I could feel its presence. Occult tradition tells us that every tree, in addition to its evolving vegetal consciousness, also has a tree spirit that looks after it. I'm not sure how much of the force of a tree is connected to its tree spirit. More about spirits and elementals shortly.

I always taught my children in school how in the winter, the life force of a tree would retreat into its roots, deep in the earth. Then in the spring, its energy would surge upward and cause the tree to come back to life. I think that's why I was so aware of the force of majestic deciduous trees. They must radiate more energy during the summer months than many of our smaller evergreen trees in California.

Of course, California has redwood trees. I was fortunate to teach school for twenty-four years in a tiny school district located in a redwood forest. Each morning, my children and I would enter a special circle of redwoods we called the sanctuary. After we were under the palpable protective influence of the trees, we would open each day with poems and morning songs.

I also taught my children the spectacular truth that without our friends the trees, there would be no life on earth. Trees breathe out oxygen and breathe in CO_2, the opposite of our human breaths. Maybe that's why it's always fun for me to find a special tree and breathe with it. Last summer, while vacationing in Seattle, Hana and I were drawn to an incredible chestnut tree in Lincoln Park in southwest Seattle.

I found the tree first and told Hana, "You have to feel the emanations of this tree."

When she came into its aura, it was like being in the presence of a spiritual master. She said, "That tree is buzzing." We both felt its tremendous vibration. On several occasions, we took advantage of this friend to meditate with our backs against its trunk. That special tree deepened our meditations exponentially. Its tree spirit no doubt assisted as well.

I mentioned how that tree felt like being in the presence of a master. Well, there are many stories about connections between spiritual figures and special trees. Again, as in the pattern of this book, rather than quote research stories of masters and their trees from the past, I will stick to my own experiences and share them. For me, my own experiences are the ones that bring spiritual principles and the world of unseen energies into my real, everyday life. I have had two of these specially blessed trees in my life.

When Meher Baba came to America in 1956, he made a stop on a mountaintop in Ojai, California. Ojai is a community just east of Santa Barbara, and ever since Annie Besant brought her theosophical group there in the 1920s, it has become a haven for all sorts of yoga, meditation, and spiritually oriented groups and teachers. In the chapter on sacred pilgrimage, I mentioned Khuldabad in India as being nicknamed the Valley of the Saints, since over seven hundred saints are buried there. Well, to me, Ojai is our American "Valley of the Saints," and I try to visit there twice a year. And it's partly because of two sacred trees.

Meher Baba spent the day at a retreat in the upper Ojai Valley. While there, he walked to the outcropping of land overlooking a spectacular vista, including Oxnard and Ventura and the distant Pacific Ocean. It was while looking at this view that he made the comment I used earlier in the chapter: "try to love [God] through nature." He then went to an incredible California live oak tree and sat down under its spreading branches. He talked to his followers for a while, perhaps enjoying the delightful canopy of branches that made a little enclosed room under the tree.

For the last fifty-eight years, this live oak tree has been referred to as "Baba's tree." Every pilgrim who comes to Meher Mount, a lovely Baba retreat in the West, visits Baba's tree. The canopy now completely touches the ground, with one "doorway" standing open. When you approach the tree, you are aware of the sanctified vibration radiating from the tree, and to sit and meditate there is to enjoy a truly holy spot.

The other tree I always visit in the Ojai Valley has to do with Jiddu Krishnamurti, another saint who lived there. I know Krishnaji's followers would never refer to him as a "saint." However, in 1967, in answer to a question by a young Western man, Meher Baba said that Krishnamurti was stationed on the fifth plane of mental consciousness. That means, according to Baba's cosmology, that Krishnaji's consciousness was one with the universal mind or, as Carl Jung would call it, fully conscious of the collective unconscious. This advanced consciousness would render K a real saint, if ever there was one.

One can read Krishnamurti's life story in any number of fascinating books. And I cannot really go into much here. However, one pivotal point in his development of advanced consciousness happened in Ojai under a California pepper tree. According to legend, Gautama Buddha achieved enlightenment while meditating under a bodhi tree, and a tree figured in Krishnamurti's unveiling as well. It was in the evening of August 20, 1922. Krishnaji had been experiencing his mysterious process for several days: pain at the nape of his neck, and it felt like "many needles" were being driven into the top of his head. He went outside his cottage and sat cross-legged in a meditation posture under a pepper tree. All of a sudden, he entered a new inner world that would leave him transformed for the rest of his life. As he put it later, "Nothing could ever be the same. I have drunk at the clear pure waters at the source of the fountain of life. ... Never can I be in utter darkness; I have seen the glorious and healing light. ... Truth has been revealed to me and the darkness has been dispersed" (Pupul Jayakar, *Krishnamurti*, p 48).

In my view, this was the moment when K broke through to the fifth plane of consciousness of the mental sphere. Such a sudden expansion of consciousness results when subtle and mental sanskaras become sufficiently balanced or burned up to reduce the veil that obscures the inner mind enough to reveal the realm of the fifth plane. This is a permanent illumination. I have visited that pepper tree many, many times in the past thirty years. And the charge radiating from the force of this tree is truly astonishing. When you sit under Krishnamurti's pepper tree and close your eyes, you really go into an instant meditation.

Before leaving the topic of Krishnamurti, one footnote: Spiritual figures also hold unseen forces, and these can often have an effect on the plant kingdom. Mark Lee tells an interesting story in his book *Knocking at the Open Door*. Once, during the 1960s, Krishnaji was visiting his school for children near Varanasi in North India. At the Rajghat-Besant School, there was a nice grove of old mango trees. K heard that the gardener was planning on cutting all the trees down because they hadn't produced fruit in some years. Krishnamurti asked the gardener to hold off on his plan for one more year. The next day, K went into the grove and had a word with those trees. He told the mango trees that they would all be cut down in a year if they didn't start producing fruit. The following year saw a bumper crop of the juiciest mangoes the trees had ever produced, and those trees continued to produce mangoes for many years to come. So not only can trees help man, but it seems that man can help trees.

The word *tree* comes from the middle English "treow" and also the old Celtic "dreu," which means "truth." The members of the ancient priest caste in England were called Druids, from the same derivation. Druids worshipped trees and especially held the oak tree sacred. This also makes me think of Norse mythology. The Norse imagined all creation to be a giant tree. In this tree were the worlds of humans, giants, and gods. This tree was named Yggdrasil. Also, the Viking Adam and Eve were trees: Ask and Embla, the ash tree and the elm tree, became the first humans, according to their mythology.

My own favorite tree is the palm tree. I remember as a child visiting my grandma in Florida and just sitting quietly under a coconut palm and being mesmerized by the wind rustling in the fronds. Palm trees also have a special spiritual significance. According to Meher Baba and others, the indwelling soul evolves consciousness in creation through incarnating in increasingly complex life forms. The palm tree is the last plant form before the evolving soul makes the leap to the insect kingdom.

One sign of the higher evolution of the palm is that it is the only tree that stands with its "head" in the air. As explained by Dr. Rudolf Steiner (and also mentioned in the medicine chapter), plants have their heads in the earth, absorbing water and nutrients. They can be compared to an upside-down human being. If you cut off branches from a tree, the tree simply grows them back. Even Krishnamurti's wonderful pepper tree was destroyed by lightning storm and almost burned back to a stump. But it slowly regenerated, and it now has a lovely canopy of new branches. A palm tree, however, will die if its top is cut off. It has made an evolutionary turn to prepare for the insect realm. According to Meher Baba, the date palm is the transitional form before insects. You can almost imagine a date wiggling away like a worm that suddenly sprouted legs or turned into a cockroach.

Trees certainly radiate a force. But a well-kept and nurtured garden can also be a serene place of bliss and tranquility. I would like to discuss the various elements you can combine to create a unique garden sanctuary in any urban or rural setting. Again, I am offering my own experience as a starting point. Feng shui, the Chinese science of placement of objects, can be a help in laying out or enhancing a garden. Feng shui suggests how energies in nature flow or radiate.

Some elements in a garden include gateways, paths, rocks, benches or chairs, and wind chimes or whirlybirds of all kinds. Flags are also a possibility. I think you can understand the types of energies you combine in a garden setting when contemplating these elements. A gateway, for example, acts as a demarcation line between the outside environment and the sanctuary energy of a garden. I have two trellis archways in my garden; one is over the pathway leading to my little meditation chapel. The archway says, "Now one is moving toward a session of meditation." The mind is already calming itself and leaving the worries of the world behind.

Flowing water, waterfalls, and fountains circulate etheric currents and refresh stagnant energy. In my garden, I have one large pond with a waterfall and two smaller fountains. I turn on the pumps whenever I have company over or spend time outside. Even the electricity operating the pumps represents circulating force. And the sound vibration we discussed in the medicine chapter can have a healing effect and encourage an alpha brain wave pattern. Some people use recordings of waterfalls (so-called white noise) to relax and fall asleep at night. I have my waterfall and pond positioned by my meditation room, so if I have the door open, I can easily hear the water.

According to Taoist philosophy, statues and stones in a garden create solidity and stability in the energy field. For people who find themselves multitasking all day, sitting in a rock garden can bring great and immediate psychological relief. In my own garden, I was very fortunate to have inherited from a friend of mine more than a dozen green jadite stones taken from riverbeds in Northern California. Two of them are massive standing stones four feet high. When I got these stones, I created a garden around them, with a pathway weaving in and out of garden mounds. The stones acted as sort of seed forms, among which I planted flowers and shrubs, with a few sacred statues thrown in.

After visiting ancient Indian ruins in the Southwest, Blake and I decided to copy the sacred design of the ritual temples called kivas. We made three garden kivas: round beds created with bricks and mortar. They turned out to be raised flower beds, not sunken Indian kivas. In the largest of the garden kivas, I used a compass to set four standing stones at the cardinal points. For two of the directions, I used semiprecious hunks of rose quartz and aventurine. In terms of the energy of the garden, drawing a personal connection created an emotional tie to the design. The idea of a kiva in a garden created a living flow of energy from my imagination to the garden.

I then used statues to complete the concept. Again, the statues create stability in the energy field and can act as a focus for human appreciation of the area's beauty. In the largest of the kivas, I placed a cement statue of Kwan Yin, the Chinese Mother Earth, right in the center of the circle. So there is the sense that Mother Earth herself is looking over the garden and its plants. In the smaller two kivas, there's a unicorn and a statue of St. Francis. These are both powerful, symbolic images for me. St. Francis was a perfect master who incarnated in the West, and the unicorn is a symbol of a spiritual teacher. So when I see these statues, my own thought-feelings blend with the flowing prana of the garden. You can begin to get a feeling of how delightfully satisfying it can be to create a personal and meaningful garden environment.

Wind chimes, whirly birds, flags, and bells are the opposite of statuary. Rather than stabilizing energy, they attract and move etheric currents. You can use feng shui principles to place both statues and wind chimes and create a balanced garden.

According to the feng shui principles of the Black Hat Tantric sect of Buddhism, the eight directions within a house or property have various psychological significance. Using a bagua, or feng shui map, you can locate areas of your living space connected, say, with career, health, money, or relationships. It's not necessary to go into great detail for the main principles to be understood. Let's say you have a job that offers you little satisfaction. You might position a wind chime or a bell in the portion of your garden related to careers. The energy of the ringing chimes would support personal growth and change. Or let's say you have a good marriage, and you want to keep it that way. On your property, in the relationship area, you could place a large decorative stone or a beautiful garden statue. In my own garden, my meditation chapel happens to be in the relationship corner. You can imagine your own interpretation using feng shui principles. But for me, such a position for meditation helps my marriage to be anchored in spiritual principles.

To really understand the spiritual forces that support plant life of all kinds in a garden, you have to journey into another realm entirely. To understand the occult reality of a beautiful garden, you have to understand the spiritual beings connected to the elements of air, earth, fire, and water: the sylphs, the gnomes, the salamanders, and the undines. In short, you have to understand the fairy kingdom.

Of course, such creatures have been the subject matter of all sorts of folktales from oral traditions all over the world. And it's easy to relegate them to the vivid imagination of a good storyteller. But occult researchers, especially in the twentieth century, surprised the world by declaring that fairy creatures were real; they were servants of the earth and carried energies in the various realms of nature. They are the worker bees of Mother Earth.

By using the tenth psychic sense, the so-called vibrational sense, you can see behind the veil of nature with clairvoyance (or clear seeing). During my period of investigating the psychic sensitivities of children, I learned that clairvoyance and the sixth sense, telepathy, are the two most common of the seven psychic senses and the abilities that are easiest to bring through to physical brain consciousness. And what do you suppose were the first things the clairvoyant children wanted to tell me about? The fairies they saw in the woods. Even my own son, Blake, saw the fairy world on a trip to Ireland when he was nine years old.

The two of us were on holiday in Ireland. We were hiking up the Tork waterfall in Killarney National Park. We sat by the falls, and I started to do my daily meditation, which I love to do in energy-charged spots in nature, which Tork waterfall especially was. Blake busied himself with tossing pebbles into the water. All of a sudden, Blake started giggling. He laughed and laughed, and then he yelled out, "Do you see them, Dad? Do you see them?" I asked him what he was talking about, and he replied, "The fairies, Dad. Do you see the water fairies? They slide down the waterfall and jump up and then slide down again and again." Then he started giggling and giggling with delight. Later, when we went back to our bed-and-breakfast, I had him draw pictures of the creatures he had seen; they were blue, fat, and shaped like raindrops. I still have that picture.

The fairy kingdom has been written about in many occult treatises. And the work these elemental creatures do in nature has long been understood by spiritual students. For further study, my favorite books are *Fairies at Work and Play* by Geoffrey Hodson and *The Real World of Fairies* by Dora Kunz (née Van Gelder), the late president of the American Section of the Theosophical Society.

Perhaps the most common place where students discuss the real world of fairies is in the spiritual community in northern Scotland, called Findhorn. I visited this special spot twice and have met four of the founders. The one collaborator I've never met was R. Ogilvie Crombie, the man who contacted the nature spirits and explained to the Findhorn Foundation how to consciously enlist the help of the fairy kingdom in growing the flowers and vegetables Findhorn is so famous for. Crombie described an encounter he had with the fairies in his *Occult Diaries*, published by Gordon Lindsay:

> [All of a sudden everything] changed and I saw the earth spirits, the elementals: the nymphs, dryads, fairies, the elves, gnomes and so on. Some of them were dancing around me in rings. All were welcoming me and full of rejoicing and delight. I was outside time, and all was happening at once. (p 122)

According to Roc (his nickname), the fairies work with the plants on the etheric or energy level. Each plant has in the etheric an archetypal pattern that guides its expansive growth. The nature spirits' task is to move energies and support this growth. In *The Real World of Fairies,* Dora Kunz (née Van Gelder) describes the work of a fairy:

> In the interchange of energies, those from the earth and from the sun, the fairy plays a definite part. He has power over both of these currents, especially the vitality from the sun. … He first of all puts himself in rapport with the plant by making his own heart center beat with the rhythm of the plant. He stands off and sizes up what he wants to do. Then he goes to work. He skips and hops all

over the plant and pats it with touches of light which flow from his own hands into the streams of the plant. In this way he alters and adjusts its life. He likes to have a gay show of flowers, and so he is likely to keep an eye on this aspect, but his main duty is to make the plant do as well as possible under existing conditions. ...

It may properly be asked, "Would plants grow without this aid?" They most certainly would, but the intervention of fairies (and the care given by human beings) makes the difference between scraggly and luxurious growth. (pp 41–42)

We can help the fairies by believing in them and by consciously inviting them into our gardens.

In my book, *The Secret Life of Kids*, I encountered many children who saw elementals in the woods. A seven-year-old named Sheri observed fairies in New Mexico, upstate New York, and India; she had some ideas concerning their work. I quote from an audiotaped interview I (J.P.) had with her in 1979 in India:

Sheri: I see fairies and elves in the woods.

J.P.: What do they look like?

Sheri: Well, which ones, the fairies or the elves?

J.P.: The fairies.

Sheri: The fairies in New Mexico look very pretty. They are dressed in white and have white wings, and they mostly have brown hair. They're about four and a half inches tall.

J.P.: What do they do?

Sheri: They like to play games. And they're always near flowers and beautiful plants. That's where I mostly see them. But fairies are up in the high places [i.e., in trees, etc.] and elves are down in the low places. Fairies can fly but elves can't.

J.P.: What colors are the elves that you see?

Sheri: Well, in India they have designed elves. They have pretty designs. But in New Mexico, they have plain colors, like green and red. In India their caps are different: They have several points with little gold balls on the end.

J.P.: What do you mean "they have designs"?

Sheri: On their shirts, their shirts are sort of light, light green with pretty designs on the front, like butterflies and stuff. They have gold shoes with little butterfly designs.

J.P.: Which are bigger, elves or fairies?

Sheri: Fairies. Elves are like only three inches tall. But the elves are fatter than the fairies. And the fairies are mostly girls.

J.P.: Can you see through them?

Sheri: Well, sometimes I can see through the fairies.

J.P.: What work do they do?

Sheri: I've seen them smell flowers. They usually just like to play, smell flowers, and sleep. They never eat, because they smell flowers.

J.P.: Are there the same types all over New Mexico?

Sheri: All over New Mexico there are the same kind, because I've seen them in Los Alamos, Albuquerque, and Las Cruces, and they're all the same kind.

J.P.: Have you seen any different kinds?

Sheri: Yes, in India and in New York, they're pretty different.

J.P.: What's different about them in New York?

Sheri: Well, they don't have any shoes, and the elves have red, like, pants outfits.

J.P.: You usually see fairies only near flowers. Do you think the flowers help them or they help the flowers, or both?

Sheri: They make the flowers prettier and nicer. They look at them and they sort of know the flowers and know what the flowers can do, and they ask the flowers to make them prettier. And by smelling them, the flowers like that, so they get prettier so more elves and fairies will smell them. (pp 70–71)

A six-year-old from Philadelphia told me, "There used to be all kinds of fairies, but some of them you never see anymore." Naturally, attracting fairies to a small garden plot in a city would offer more of a challenge than to call them to help in a rural garden. I also think the artificial electromagnetic grid we have created, with all our ubiquitous wireless devices, probably does not encourage the elementals. I've even read that nature spirits will not help enliven genetically modified food, because the plants that have been modified have very little life force. The gardeners at Findhorn recommend that you keep a corner of the garden in a wild, unkempt state. This corner will become the elemental headquarters, from which the workers will venture out into the more civilized portions of the garden.

I also use another trick to attract the fairies to my garden. In a shady spot, I created a miniature fairy garden. With stones, shells, three model fairy houses, and little ceramic and metal fairies, I made a little fairy village. I also made a spiral design out of pebbles, which is the symbol of Mother Earth in Peru. When I visited Machu Picchu, I became very interested in the worship of Pachamama, the Peruvian Mother Earth. So in my fairy garden, I honor Pachamama by having her symbol, the spiral, prominently featured. I love my fairy garden, though I do not know if it actually attracts real fairies.

When discussing the unseen forces alive in a garden, we must again return to the work of Rudolf Steiner. Farmers came to Dr. Steiner and asked, "Tell us, what do your spiritual-scientific theories say about helping me grow healthier and more nutritional crops?" Spiritual law compelled him through the questions of his students to delve into the topic of agriculture. During 1923 and 1924, Dr. Steiner discussed fertilizers, pest control, companion plants, harvesting, and so on with groups of farmers. These discussions soon developed into what we call today biodynamic agriculture.

Biodynamic gardening is a huge topic, and rather than offer research into its principles, I'll just mention a few aspects of this approach that I understand and try to utilize. Dr. Steiner discussed how plants are intimately connected with the earth, sun, stars, animals, and human beings. You might say plants are part of the unified geosphere, and to be a gardener or farmer, you have to learn to balance the occult and physical forces of all these realms. The fruits and vegetables grown in such a holistic, conscious environment have more nutritional life force, according to Dr. Steiner. For example, Dr. Steiner said the manure used for fertilizing and composting should be from animals that live on your own land. This connects the local etheric earth forces with the soul of the plants.

In my chapter on water, I discussed Dr. Steiner's cow-horn fertilizer mixture; stuffing a cow horn with manure and planting it in the earth for the whole of the winter electrified the manure with earth radiations that could then charge water to become a super fertilizer in the garden. Dr. Steiner discussed complex astrological issues a biodynamic farmer should take into consideration, along with issues like companion plants growing near each other.

Due to the occult complexities of this approach, I have only incorporated a few biodynamic principles into my own gardening. In my composting, for instance, I ordered biodynamic compost starter from the Josephine Porter Institute in Virginia. I also try to start my compost using some locally grown cow pies from our Walnut Creek hills. One winter, I went to a butcher shop and got a cow horn to bury with manure.

Stinging nettles feature strongly into biodynamics. Nettles are filled with more etheric forces than most other plants. This force can be utilized in a healthy garden. To make easy supercharged fertilizer, take several nettle plants and soak them in a bucket of water for a week. Then you can take homeopathic portions of the water to mix in a watering can. Thus, a bucket of water can be used for weeks in your garden.

Just as with our fairy friends, I don't believe you necessarily need to know the details of biodynamics. The living imagination within the mind of a gardener concerning the forces of the seasons, the phases of the moon, the work of the plants living in balance between earth and sun helps to raise consciousness. And, as in all phases of life, trying to be aware or mindful of the workings of unseen forces in life makes gardening more interesting and satisfying.

The final topic I wish to examine in this chapter is flowers. In my own garden, I found that critters of all kinds liked to eat the vegetables and fruits I tried to grow. Since organically grown fruits and vegetables are so plentiful in California (and relatively cheap as well), I decided to focus my gardening effort on flowers. Not only is the beautiful color, form, and scent of the flowers delightful, but I believe there are deeper, more spiritual dimensions to these special gifts of Mother Nature. Dr. Steiner, in a lecture to doctors, discussed flowers. Doctors had to understand the plants from which medications in his anthroposophical approach to healing were formulated: "Don't look at flowers in such an abstract way, and don't just make abstract images and concept of them, but have the true, beautiful sense for the soul spiritual quality dwelling in flowers" (*Who Was Ita Wegman?*, vol 2, p 10).

In the next chapter, we'll see how Dr. Edward Bach recognized the special qualities of flowers and developed homeopathic flower remedies to treat certain emotional problems. To learn more about the inner nature of flowers, we have to turn from the West to the East. Sri Aurobindo was a great spiritual master who lived in Pondicherry, in south India, during the first half of the twentieth century. His companion, who handled the practical aspects of their ashram, was a French woman Aurobindo referred to as the Mother. The Mother had an extremely intimate relationship with flowers. Flowers were her friends; she could blend her consciousness with them and learn the quality or mission of each species of flower. This she shared in her book *Flowers and Their Messages*.

For one thing, she said, flowers have the ability to hold a vibration from one human being and carry this vibration to another human being. So when you give a bouquet of flowers on Valentine's Day to your loved one, the flowers can transmit your loving thoughts in far more than a symbolic way.

But, in addition, flowers carry their own energy, their own message:

> [When the higher mind] manifests as a plant, in the form
> of a flower, it's in the form of a wordless prayer. It is the
> clear aspiration of the plant toward the divine. (p 111)

How can you identify the quality each flower manifests? The Mother answered this way:

> If you are in contact with [the flower]. If you feel it. You can get an impression which may be translated as a thought. This is how I give a meaning to flowers and plants. There is a kind of identification with the vibration—a perception of the quality that it represents. (p vi)

Some examples of the energy flowers hold are as follows:

- A golden, yellow hibiscus shows the power of the supramental mind.
- Coreopsus is cheerfulness in work for the divine.
- Pink roses are perfect surrender.
- Red petunias are joyful, physical enthusiasm.
- Jasmine is purity.

I think of these qualities in much the way that I imagine the fairy kingdom at work in the garden. The currents of the mind follow interest. And the presence of unseen energy in the garden renders work in the garden and enjoyment of it a much more satisfying and almost spiritual endeavor.

An elderly Buddhist priest in Japan was watering his irises with such tender care and devotion that those observing him asked him why. "One day," the priest replied, "these flowers will also be Buddhas." Caring for a garden, just like caring for animals or children, is caring and nurturing our younger brothers on this path to the divine.

The deeper, symbolic meaning of gardening lies in a mystical conception. The real garden actually exists within. And watering, fertilizing, and weeding the inner garden of the mind is treading the spiritual path. You have to water and encourage the good thoughts and impulses, and try to weed out the negative ones. Thus, you can become a true gardener in every realm of creation.

CHAPTER 12

Medicine

The universe and everything in it, including human beings, is energy—energy on the physical level, emotional level, and mental level. In this book, the focus has been on recognizing and utilizing the energies not so easily perceived on the physical plane. These nonphysical energies, whose source is on the inner planes, I have referred to as prana, life force, or etheric energy.

In the chapter on water, it was very clear in Dr. Emoto's work that even thought energy, thinking, can affect and change physical matter. You may recall that if you think or say "I love you" to a glass of water, the frozen crystals of water form beautiful snowflake-like hexagonal crystals. However, if you say or think "I hate you" to that same sample of water, the crystals are lopsided, distorted, and discolored.

The field of holistic energy medicine is another realm wherein the existence of undetected occult energies can and do affect tissue in the physical body. In this chapter, as well as in the section on education and child-rearing, my emphasis will be a little more in the direction of persuasion. I believe allopathic medicine, particularly in its reliance on pharmaceutical substances, often does harm to the balanced, physical energy matrix.

My brother Tom and I have polycystic kidney disease (PKD), an inherited disease in which inoperable cysts grow on the kidneys. Madame H. P. Blavatsky and the spiritually oriented poet Emily Dickinson both died of PKD. Tom recently sent me a new link to a promising new drug for PKD. The tract said, "This drug can significantly retard the growth of cysts, particularly in 19- to 49-year-olds." The only two disadvantages are that you can only take the drug for thirty days, and the serious side effects include liver failure. Energy medicine differs in its approach to health and illness because it does not involve dangerous and untested pharmaceuticals.

There are many, many different choices in the alternative medical arena. The three most well-known and most practiced in the United States are homeopathy, traditional Chinese medicine, and Ayurvedic medicine. I'm not planning on discussing Ayurveda, because I have not had personal experiences with that holistic approach, and this book is not concerned with research but rather with my own experiences and understandings.

A personal anecdote, in fact, may be the best way to start. I live in an area said to have so many pollens in springtime that even people who move here who have never been troubled with spring hay fever will get symptoms within five years. I never had any allergies, so I did not believe that prediction. But sure enough, during my fifth spring in Contra Costa County, I developed hay fever symptoms of itchy eyes, sneezing, and a runny nose. I was miserable for around two or three months each spring.

Two years later, I discovered a Swiss homeopathic product by A. Vogal called Pollinosan. You start by taking ten drops a day, two months prior to allergy season. That year—and every year since—I have been symptom-free during the hay fever months, March through May. I have recommended Pollinosan to many friends, and it works similarly for everyone. As my brother Roger used to say, you can't argue with success.

Dr. Amit Goswami, in his book *The Quantum Doctor,* has a similar story:

> I was a 12-year-old kid, popular and active in sports, good in academics, but I was hugely unhappy because I had an utterly embarrassing thing happening to my body: warts. And they grew everywhere on my body. We tried various wart-removing agents, but nothing worked. Finally, somebody suggested homeopathy. I still remember the medicine I got—Thuja 30X, four little white globules that tasted sweet. I had to suck on them until they dissolved in my mouth. After two days, one by one, warts just fell off

my body. … I was cured. I was so relieved. It was miracle medicine. (p 153)

My wife also has a homeopathy story. When she was living in Washington DC, around the year 2000, the office where she worked was being remodeled: new carpeting, wallpaper, and paint. The fumes of the chemicals involved sent Hana's body into a severe allergic shock. She lost all her energy, and her skin turned almost greenish. She was confined to bed by her doctors while on workers' compensation. But her allopathic doctors could do nothing to help her.

Finally, she heard of a doctor who used Chinese acupuncture and homeopathic remedies. Hana was prescribed fifteen homeopathic remedies to take three times a day. In two days, all the toxic allergic symptoms were gone, and she felt good. In two months, she felt better than she had ever felt in her life.

Homeopathy is founded on two principles. One is a reasonable and almost acceptable idea to an allopathic physician. But the other makes no sense unless you take occult forces into account. The first axiom of homeopathy is that "Like cures like." If a certain substance will cause an array of symptoms in a healthy body, then that same substance will become a cure in a diseased body showing the same symptoms. This is a bit like the allopathic principle of vaccinations. A "like" substance prevents a "like" disease.

In the Dark Ages of Europe, the old crone or healer of a village used the same principle intuitively. If there were a battle and the healer needed to treat a wounded man, she would go to the battlefield and collect herbs to mix with healing poultices or drinks. Somehow, the wounds were connected to the like herbs.

The other axiom of homeopathy is much more esoteric. It is the concept that "Less is more." The more you dilute a substance in water, using specific procedures, the more potent it becomes. Let's say one part of that medicine is diluted with nine parts of a water-alcohol mixture. This is shaken in a special way—different homeopaths use different procedures— then nine parts of the "potentized substance" is discarded, and the one part that remains is again diluted and shaken with nine more parts of alcohol-water. This process is repeated as many times as you like, to get tinctures of 1X, 10X, or 100X.

As I've already mentioned, I have polycystic kidney disease. I have inoperable cysts in my kidneys that pose no health risk unless they grow and eventually cut off kidney function. I'm not too worried about them because I'm seventy-three years old, and the cysts are still tiny. They like to grow and feed off animal protein, and I've been a vegetarian for forty-seven years. That has helped the kidney cysts to stay small, according to my doctor.

Back in the 1920s, Dr. Rudolf Steiner developed two homeopathic remedies for polycystic kidneys. I take these two medicines daily. One is Renes Veratrum; it contains (among other substances) veratrum *e rad* 6X and *renes* 7X. The other remedy is Cuprum Stannum, which contains (among other things) *stannum metallicum* 3X and *cuprum metallicum* 8X.

I told my brother, who also has polycystic kidney disease, about these two effective homeopathic remedies, and he, a scientist who works for the government, laughed at me. He said that by the time homeopathic medicines are diluted, there is sometimes not even one molecule of the original so-called medicine. What incredible nonsense that using such a substance could do anything! He merely chalked it up to his gullible brother falling for another ridiculous New Age fad.

According to Dr. Steiner, who adapted homeopathic cures into his particular approach to medicine, the more a substance is diluted and shaken, the more etheric energy from the original plant mixture is released. Thus, a 30X mixture is a highly potentized medication with specific etheric forces. And these specific energies are created to focus on specific bodily conditions. There is an etheric web around each of us that forms the matrix of energies that holds the patterns for the tissue of the physical body. In the anthroposophical process of creating homeopathic remedies, the inherent substances are practically reduced to pure etheric force so that, when ingested, the energized cure works directly on the etheric counterpart of physical tissue. As Dr. Goswami says in *The Quantum Doctor,* the etheric body is "the morphogenic field that shapes living forms" (p 267).

I will admit that the homeopathic medical approach, in my own experience, seems to be far better at treating chronic rather than acute health issues. In India in 1975, I had flu-like symptoms. A homeopathic follower of the master Meher Baba, named Padri, treated me with small homeopathic pills. He assured me I'd be fine. Eight hours later, I became very sick with the flu, which unfortunately occurred just before my twenty-four-hour plane ride back to America. However, when I take my homeopathic remedy for hay fever one month prior to allergy season, it always keeps me symptom-free all spring.

By far, the most articulate and interesting approach to energy medicine to me is the approach Dr. Steiner developed in the early 1920s. Dr. Steiner was also a spiritual teacher who worked within the Anthroposophical Society, headquartered in Dornach, Switzerland. Dr. Steiner's teaching impulses would very often originate in questions from all kinds of his students. Thus, when farmers asked how occult science affected the earth and growing plants, Dr. Steiner would lecture on farming; he also developed what he called biodynamic agriculture. Or when educators asked him about how his philosophy impacted growing children, the resulting teachings led to Waldorf education.

The same process occurred with physicians. Dr. Steiner developed two ways of explaining to doctors how occult energies worked through the physical body. These are called the threefold man and the fourfold man.

In the threefold approach, the body is divided into three portions: the metabolic-limb system, the nerve-sense system, and the rhythmic system. The metabolic-limb system is seen as a "hot," mobile part of the body and includes the digestive organs and the reproductive organs. This system is the most unconscious but is also the most active. Metabolism is in constant motion to keep the body energized and healthy, but you are not consciously aware of its workings. If the system becomes cold or too still, disease or ill health results in symptoms like constipation. Dr. Steiner often recommended treating metabolic problems with homeopathic medicines or herbal drinks that are processed through the stomach and intestines.

The nerve-sense system is the opposite extreme in the body. The senses are focused in the head. The head, as opposed to the abdomen, is the most fully conscious part of the body. While the metabolic-limb system likes movement, the head system likes stillness. In fact, jarring or sudden movements of the head result in a concussion or dizziness. Sleep issues, depression, or anxiety have to do with the functioning of the nerve-sense system, which Dr. Steiner often treated with herbal baths or compresses.

The head also is cold, and when there is too much heat in this area, you are ill with a fever. A general principle would be when the head forces become too strong and overpower the metabolic system, you have a hardening or sclerotic condition. If the metabolic forces become too strong, you have inflammation.

The third bodily system exists between the two extremes of the nerve-sense system and the metabolic system. This third system is not too cold and not too hot. It is not always moving, and it's not always still. This is called the rhythmic system and consists of the heart, lungs, and circulatory system. These organs are characterized by rhythmic beating of the heart and the constant rhythm of breath. When the rhythms become upset, too slow or too fast or arrhythmic, you have illness. High blood pressure or low blood pressure can both be dangerous. Steiner treated many issues in the rhythmic system with injections that pass right into the circulating blood.

And in analyzing plants and herbs in relation to treatments for various illnesses, Steiner pointed out that a plant corresponds to an inverted human being. Thus, the roots of potatoes and carrots are used to treat nerve-sense issues. The leaves of plants like spinach and digitalis are used for imbalances in the rhythmic system. And flowers (chamomile, broccoli, etc.) can settle an upset stomach in the metabolic system.

Many methods of treating imbalances use this concept of the threefold man. The general principle, however, is that if forces in the metabolic-limb system become too strong, you have inflammation. When forces of the hard, cold, more deadened nerve-sense system become too strong, you have conditions of sclerosis.

However, another philosophical view of a human being offers a different perspective on health and healing. Readers of this book are familiar with this angle. Dr. Steiner discussed in numerous books and lectures how the human energy system is composed of different energy fields or sheaths. He called them the physical body, the etheric body, the astral body, and the ego organization (which I term the subtle and mental sheaths).

According to this Western occult view of the human being, diseases can originate in any of these four energy fields and should be treated differently according to the level where the problem exists. For example, I recently had a bicycle accident and broke my little finger. A broken bone is obviously a problem originating in the physical body, and the treatment required an operation to insert physical pins to hold the bones together and a physical cast to immobilize the finger while it healed.

It's a bit harder to understand astral or etheric health issues. Steiner said that the tendency of astral matter is to contract and to create a firm edge to its field. The etheric body, however, has the tendency to expand (as seen, for example, in the plant kingdom). So the etheric body is always pushing against the astral membrane, which holds the etheric energies in check.

I'll give you an example. A woman I knew wanted to have a baby, but she kept having miscarriages. She went to Robert Gorter, an anthroposophical doctor who was visiting San Francisco from Holland. Dr. Gorter said that the woman's astral body did not penetrate into her reproductive system fully, so she couldn't "hold" the baby. To bring the needed astrality down into the lower portion of her body, the doctor instructed her husband to use a salve made of copper and rub the ointment daily on the soles of her feet. The husband had to massage the lotion in with a figure-eight pattern. The next time she became pregnant, she successfully gave birth to a healthy baby boy.

I don't pretend to understand how these Steiner doctors diagnose occult origins of disease. They undergo eleven years of allopathic medical training and then four more years in an anthroposophical hospital, which are common in parts of Europe. They are trained to recognize how the astral and etheric forces function in health and disease.

Another example is a treatment I heard about for children with bedwetting issues. Bedwetting means the etheric body is working too strongly in the child, who can't hold back the forces of the kidney system. One treatment calls for exercises using Steiner's movement art called curative eurythmy. The child works with a trained therapist and makes various gestures with the arms, indicating the sound for the consonant B. This B sound makes a space in the air as if you were holding an etheric baby. Repetition of this gesture helps to train the child's etheric energies to hold back and be more controlled. Thus, the bedwetting comes to an end.

Of course, the principles of anthroposophical medicine are endlessly complicated. But what I most appreciate about this approach is that its practitioners consciously and purposefully take into account many levels of spiritual, occult, and living energies to diagnose and treat illness.

The premise of this book is that the world around us and our own inner structures are composed of many more diverse forces besides physical atoms. In becoming conscious of these unseen energies, we can live a more full, balanced, and enjoyable life. And anthroposophical medicine fully understands and utilizes all of these inner foundational forces of life to help the body maintain balanced health in a hectic world.

Live energies in medicine are not something invented by Dr. Steiner in 1921. For thousands of years, Taoist practitioners of traditional Chinese medicine have understood that unseen etheric energies must be clearly understood to treat illnesses. I found an excellent summary of principles of Chinese medicine in a book called *Religions* by Philip Wilkinson. Here's the way he puts it:

> For a person to be healthy, energy or chi must flow steadily along a series of meridians (channels) in the body. When disease blocks this flow, various forms of Chinese medicine can help to release it. In acupuncture and reflexology, for example, the practitioner presses certain points on the body, which restores the free flow of chi along the meridians. Getting this flow right—that is, free and in balance—fosters both physical and mental wellbeing and promotes longevity. (p 254)

Of course, this chi is simply the Taoist word for etheric formative forces discussed throughout this book. Chinese medicine recognizes two forms of chi: active (or yang) and receptive (or yin). Intertwined with the philosophy of Chinese medicine is the concept of fields of the etheric energy correlating with the five elements: earth, water, fire, metal, and wood. And each element has a yin and a yang aspect. Physical organs correspond to each type of energy as well. The yin organs are basically container organs, which store substances: the liver, heart, spleen, lungs, and kidneys. The yang organs are characterized by constant movement of substances; they are the organs of transfer: stomach, small intestines, bladder, large intestines, and gallbladder.

A full treatment of Chinese medical theory is beyond the bounds of this book and beyond my expertise.

I know that the ancient techniques of correcting imbalances of the fluid, morphogenetic etheric field through Chinese medicine has been of tremendous help to myself and many, many of my friends. And Chinese practitioners are easier to find in the United States than, say, a good anthroposophical doctor. Plus, with the long history of Chinese medicine, some of its practices—primarily herbs and acupuncture—have been recognized as valid by Western allopathic authorities.

It might be interesting to discuss times in my own life when I turned to Chinese medicine for personal health issues. When I first became a Sufi student in 1970, the health of our teacher, who was seventy-five, was being supported by Chinese herbs prepared by Dr. James Wong. I had a pulse diagnosis by him, and he said the nerves going into my heart were not working right. So I began an herbal remedy he called "triple warmer." I took this herb daily for the next ten years.

In the 1970s, I attended a weekend conference in San Francisco on traditional Chinese medicine. Since I was prone to occasional migraine headaches, I took a headache workshop. It was very helpful. Among the tips given were two that have helped me down through the years. When the migraine aura (a vision distortion) comes on, the workshop speaker said to focus all your chi on your hands and feet. This practice will help take the energy away from the head and will help nip the migraine in the bud. The other suggestion to ward off a migraine was to smell mustard. So whenever I feel a migraine coming, I open a jar of mustard and sniff it for five minutes. That often staves off the coming migraine.

In Dr. Steiner's system, a headache affects the nerve-sense system. So both migraine remedies are sensual—particularly smelling mustard. Recently, I began taking Chinese herbs again. As I mentioned, I have incurable, inherited polycystic kidney disease. I explored alternative remedies and go to Dr. Angela Tu for Chinese treatments. She gives me an herb that will strengthen my kidneys but does not cure the disease. Keeping the cysts from growing is all I need, since I still have 100 percent kidney function at age seventy-three.

In my own exploration of alternative approaches to health, I discovered another interesting type of treatment using gemstone energy, propounded by Michael Katz. I discussed his work in my chapter on the mineral kingdom. Katz basically reports that the varying etheric energies locked in the high-quality gems and crystals positively and therapeutically affect the morphogenic energy field of a human etheric body:

> Wearing a therapeutic gemstone necklace allows the gem's healing energy to penetrate the deepest level of the wearer's physical and energy dimensions. There, the gem's energy goes to work dissolving energy blockages and producing beneficial changes in the body, mind, and emotions. (*Gemstone Energy Medicine,* p 4)

I mentioned that I broke a finger in a bicycle accident. Katz writes that the energy of the gem apatite channels energy into the skeletal system. So I have been wearing my apatite necklace and carrying a one-inch-diameter apatite sphere in my pocket.

My attitude towards various therapeutic treatments is that all life is energy and that all physical forms are held together with energy. In fact, as Meher Baba says, all physical matter is simply "consolidated energy." So in seeking out treatment for any medical issue, utilizing energy-based protocols can't hurt. My broken finger certainly wasn't cured by apatite crystals. The energies coming from gemstones are too weak and subtle to bring about dramatic cures. But no doubt those energies can and do support the healing process. And even if it's just a placebo effect, I felt good integrating gemstone energy into my finger therapy. My anthroposophical doctor, Philip Incao, just emailed me that another great way to encourage circulation in my broken finger is to allow it to be stung by live stinging nettle plants. Now *there's* a therapy my Kaiser doctor didn't think of!

One medical procedure created by an acquaintance of mine, Dora Kunz, relies solely on the energy exchange between the therapist and the patient. This is called "therapeutic touch." Dora Kunz was a clairvoyant, trained in the Theosophical Society by the renowned seer C. W. Leadbeater. In the 1980s, Dora became the president of the American Section of the Theosophical Society. But her major life work was developing, with her friend Delores Krieger, this promising form of energy medicine. In the therapeutic touch approach, the therapist electrifies the palms of the hands with etheric, vital force and then passes the palms over the diseased organ of the patient. The organ then gets a dosage of the therapist's own vitality, which has a healing effect.

Of course, everyone has heard of the "laying on of hands." Teachers from Jesus to Krishnamurti have used the energized touch of the hand to heal. There are two aspects of therapeutic touch that are truly unique.

First, Dora, as a trained clairvoyant, was able to see just how the energy field was working in her patients. That way, she could teach others how and where to pass their hands to have the desired effect. Obviously, most of us are not clairvoyant. But we must act as if we are conscious of the invisible effects our thoughts, words, and deeds have on others. It's the same with anthroposophical doctors. They're not clairvoyantly seeing the astral and etheric bodies, but knowing the principles of these energy fields, they act as if they are seeing them.

Second, and more surprisingly, therapeutic touch has actually caught on in allopathic settings. Thousands of nurses have been trained to use Dora's techniques in hospitals around the country. The reason: It has been scientifically proven to work.

Another healer I'm familiar with used his electrified hands to heal thousands of people. He was the cofounder of the Theosophical Society, Colonel Henry S. Olcott. Col. Olcott healed thousands during trips through India in the 1880s. He would touch people's limbs or heads and say in Hindi, "Be healed." And they were. He also would use a silver tube to blow on the affected area or into a glass of water and have the patient drink from the energized water.

After seven years of doing these energy healings, Col. Olcott had to stop. He was beginning to suffer from personal health issues. During his healing work, he was actually transferring some of his own personal vitality to each patient. Such a process cannot go on for long before the healer himself becomes ill.

Myofascial release (MFR) is another interesting approach, developed by John Barnes, PT. Fascia is connective tissue penetrating all parts of your body—no doubt related to what I would term the etheric body or etheric web. When there is trauma—physical or emotional—or inflammation, the fasciae can be restricted, putting pressure on nerves, muscles, or blood vessels, thereby also restricting the flow of chi or etheric vitality. Barnes said that accidents or emotional trauma can restrict fascia, and through gentle treatments, "unwinding" can take place. Unwinding is when stuck or locked energy is released from restriction in the fascia, and the patient may actually relive an accident or, say, a childhood emotional trauma.

My wife, an MFR practitioner, was releasing a scar connected with my broken finger caused by the bike accident. While she was working, I relived the accident and knew all of a sudden exactly where and how I had hit the ground. Previously, I had no recollection of the precise experience of the accident. I "saw" myself hitting my shoulder, which had been causing me a lot of pain but had been undiagnosed by my doctor.

When Hana does her myofascial release work, she always puts on soft music and an aromatic scent disperser. Relaxation and healing are connected to all the senses, and a good healer will activate as many healing channels as possible.

Sound and music have been used for thousands of years to heal human energy imbalances. In my forty-two years of teaching schoolchildren, I have made frequent use of bells and a small, seven-stringed lyre. By introducing a bell sound to a classroom of children, they catch the vibration and quickly become attentive in order to hear it. Every parent can use bells and music in child-rearing, a topic I'll discuss in the next chapter.

In regard to medicine, I have experimented with sound vibration through an approach called "acutonics," espoused by Donna Carey and Ellen Franklin. In acutonics, the practitioner uses tuning forks against bone to bring precise, calibrated frequencies into the body. The forks ring with sound energy, accessing the energy meridians of the body via specific acupuncture points. I have used various tuning forks for self-healing, too. By hitting a fork and pressing the handle end to an aching muscle, I have found the sound vibration can help in relieving pain.

I remember meeting Steven Halpern in the 1980s. He also works with sound and healing. Lying on the floor and listening to his *Spectrum Suite* is an amazing experience. The tones he plays on his synthesizer are attuned to each chakra of the body. And the *Spectrum Suite* stimulates each chakra one by one, right up the body. You feel relaxed yet energized after listening to it. I wonder how a materialist would explain the very definite stimulation of the chakra sites in the body with Halpern's sound composition.

In this exciting age of descendant spirituality, many, many medical practitioners are experimenting with different innovative energy approaches to health and healing. Just attend a New Life Health and Healing Expo to become acquainted with a sampling of such approaches.

My general guideline has been to share information that I personally understand from my experiences over the last fifty years. In this book, I cannot cover everything. I will end this survey of New Age medicine, therefore, with a look at Bach Flower Remedies.

I began this chapter by reminding the reader of Dr. Emoto's remarkable work with the energizing of water in his laboratories in Japan. It would be an easy step for such a scientist to understand Dr. Edward Bach's astonishing work in England during the 1930s. Dr. Bach was a homeopath, but he was not satisfied with the process of treating physical ailments with the homeopathic preparations made from minerals and herbs.

The 1930s was a decade of psychology. Through the work of Freud, Jung, Adler, and others, people were tracing many of their illnesses to buried psychological trauma. Bach thought there must be some way to alleviate psychological and emotional conditions. He began to experiment with plants—particularly the most highly developed portion of the plant, the flower. Through a fascinating blend of using his intuition, plus trial and error, Bach experimented on himself and colleagues to discover what emotional conditions each species of flower was connected to.

Dr. Steiner explained that the plant world thrives because of strong etheric forces. The etheric body of a plant expands according to etheric laws, and this expansion is not held back by the contracting forces of an articulated astral counterpart found with animal and human forms. Therefore, the etheric forces of plants, and in Bach's case, flowers, can be used to supercharge water.

Bach developed a method to create his remedies that is simple for a student of the occult to understand. He would float flower heads in pure water and in direct sunlight for three hours. The heat of the sun transfers the etheric energy released by the flower head into the water. Bach would then mix the energized water with equal parts of brandy. This created what he referred to as the "mother tincture." This tincture he would further dilute with brandy to make the final flower remedy. Today, these general guidelines are used by many companies around the world to produce various brands of the original Bach remedies. Here are some examples of the focus of various flow remedies:

- holly—helps the patient deal with envy and jealousy
- honeysuckle—alleviates the tendency of someone who lives too much in the past
- rock rose—helps you to deal with fear

My favorite remedy is a composite one called Rescue Remedy. It's a perfect traveling companion. When I've been driving in other countries, making wrong turns while searching for a restaurant or an out-of-the-way hotel, a few drops of Rescue Remedy can alleviate tension when my nerves are frazzled. It would be great for kindergarten teachers who are overwhelmed by a fidgety group of children.

From the perspective of energy medicine, really, the sky is the limit. As we move into the new age, wellness clinics will treat virtually every illness with new energy approaches. And, when used appropriately, allopathic, Western medicine will be right there in the mix.

CHAPTER 13

Education and Child-Rearing

The considerations of this chapter are radically different from the other topics I've written about. They're almost fundamentally opposite. The other chapters have been about how recognizing, understanding, and feeling the effect of inner energies and forces from other realms enhances our well-being, health, and happiness in our everyday lives. These considerations are connected to yourself and the quality of life. Isn't it interesting for me to know how these energies work?

This chapter is solely about understanding this to help others—specifically, our dearest younger brothers and sisters on this earth: our children, who we must nurture and protect. You cannot comprehend how children grow and develop without knowing when and how their inner membranes of consciousness release mental and emotional forces. You can only understand correct timing and approaches to education by grasping how these inner forces are nurtured, channeled, and released. And you can only protect the delicate matrix of the child's nervous system and etheric web from harsh and harmful occult influences if you understand how energies work in children and what they need to be protected from.

The way these unseen forces from the inner planes affect children and activate phases of development is my field of expertise. I've been writing about it for forty years and published *The Secret Life of Kids* in 1987. Yet, interestingly, this is practically the last chapter I'm working on for this present book. I suppose, when I retired from my forty-two-year career of teaching small children, I was much more interested in writing about other topics. But now, it's time to tackle this crucial subject.

Before we can understand children, we must do a little metaphysical review. Meher Baba explained that mind consolidates into energy, and energy consolidates into matter. As individualized souls journey through lifetime after lifetime on earth, they accumulate sanskaras or impressions of all the mental, emotional, and physical experiences they undergo. Sanskaras are coded light units of mind, holding tremendous energy of life experience in latent form. When it's time for the cosmic being of a soul to be incarnated as a child on earth, the entire process is precipitated through sanskaras seeking to be re-expressed as their conditioning dictates.

I described this entire process in *The Secret Life of Kids*. It's interesting to me that these descriptions of the incarnating child still hold up, even after thirty years of further study.

The story begins when the timing is appropriate for an individual human atma (or soul) to reincarnate on the physical plane. The process proceeds gradually and in stages. First, a subgroup of the myriad individual sanskaras (impressions)—those coded units of light that form our causal body—separate and descend into partial expression in the more energized field of the *kama manas* (the subtle body). But that sanskaric cluster within the kama manas represents the germinal roots of all thoughts, feelings, words, and deeds slated for potential expression within the context of the specific karma of the coming incarnation.

As these sanskaras gather and organize energy within the structure and pattern of the kama manas, desire is born. When latent sanskaras, or impressions from the past, are infused with energy, the result is desire—the desire for expression, for manifestation in earthly life, the field in which the sanskaras were originally generated. Sanskaras provide impetus behind the repetition of previous actions, feelings, or thoughts. Because these actions, feelings, and thoughts represent blends of subtle energy that arose from physical expression in the physical world, the desire or tendency of the sanskaras is for expression in the physical sphere. The energy generated at this level, therefore, is the impulse to incarnate. It is a living force that propels an individual into the coming life.

In the meantime, the future parents, according to the dictates of karma, have prepared the fertilized egg within the protective womb of the mother. At this time, the atma makes its initial contact with the zygote, sending a beam of light through all the planes of consciousness, ending in a spinning etheric disc. This disc sets up an individual pattern of energy, magnetically attracting forces from all realms of existence to build up the future vehicles for the incarnating child (Bendit, *The Etheric Body of Man*, 1977, p 45). In some esoteric systems, this spiritual beam of living energy is called the "heart." It is a structure that will continue to form the core of the individual's being throughout that incarnation on earth. In a sense, this heart is the connecting channel between the causal body, the subtle body, and the physical body. It is a sort of elevator of consciousness along which higher, spiritual forces can be transmitted into lower levels, and through which your earthly consciousness can become aware of higher forces through spiritual progress.

As the physical body grows within the womb of the mother, etheric matter is simultaneously gathered and organized into the matrix of a new etheric body, and astral matter is similarly coalesced in a new astral vehicle. Since the sanskaric forces dictating these growth processes are descending from the levels of the causal and subtle bodies, they are first materialized in astral matter and then transmitted to the etheric and physical counterparts. These three, the astral, etheric, and physical, work as a unit; they are the vehicles of incarnation. They represent the personality or ego working within the domain of matter. However, although they work in close harmony with each other, their patterns of growth are different, and their functions within the consciousness of a human being are very specialized.

The physical body is able to take on its individual characteristics because of the sanskaric forces transmitted through the astral and etheric membranes. It undergoes the most concentrated and rapid growth in the early years of a child's life. The mature functioning of the astral and etheric bodies represents the more subjective aspects of mentality, and these subtler bodies are developed later in the child's life, even as these aspects of consciousness were developed later in the evolution of human consciousness. The physical body, which was brought to perfection earliest in the history of humanity, is the vehicle most easily available for the incarnating child to influence and use (Heindel, *The Rosicrucian Principles of Child Training*, 1928, pp 6–7). So when the physical body is released from the protective womb of the mother, most of the forces working through the astral and etheric planes are focused into processes of physical growth.

This concludes my description of these incarnating processes from my 1987 book. The whole process of birth, growth, and development of a child is based on energies from inner layers of a child's personality, working in and through the physical vehicle. In the early years, the child needs the support of the mother's energies. In fact, it is said that during the first four years of life, a child is actually psychically connected to the mother's aura and therefore, in a way, is not independent at all.

I would like to add a footnote here before we continue to consider further development of a child's consciousness. We all know that these incarnational energies sometimes fail to develop correctly, and the incarnation of a child is not successful. There can be miscarriages or premature births, and premature births often result in premature deaths. How can you understand such events from a spiritual perspective?

Again, I'll share my own experiences, which, though sad, were at the same time very illuminating. My wife and I had a premature boy, born in 1986, whose name was Whitney. He lived for only four days. While we were sharing his short life with him, I had a phone call while in the neonatal unit of the hospital. It was my spiritual teacher, Dr. James MacKie. The call came after Whitney's brain started to hemorrhage, and it was clear the angel of death was hovering close by.

I was told to touch and massage Whitney all over his body for as long as we could before he died. When he incarnated with us, apparently, he never planned on staying. Murshid told me Whitney had joined a group of workers on the astral plane, but his astral body had started to disintegrate, as happens in the after-death state. The only way he could garner the energy to create a new astral sheath to continue his work was to incarnate on earth, form a new astral membrane, and then shed the physical body. So to continue his work, he was born to die. The touching of his physical body before he died helped him gather earth forces to propel him back into the astral world.

So even tragic losses can have meaning when understood from an inner perspective. The hidden side of life is complicated and fascinating.

The whole process of birth, growth, and development of a child is based on energies from the inner layers of a child's personality, working in and through the physical vehicle. Particularly during the first seven years, the etheric formative forces have not interconnected or been released as a mature, independent layer of the child's mentality. And because this independent force field has not developed into the articulated etheric web of a mature human being, the child can experience impressions from astral realms, such as clairvoyant perceptions of the astral, telepathy, or even remembering past lives.

Also, this loosely connected energy body leaves children terribly vulnerable to the psychic forces around them. That is why parents and educators must learn how to protect small children from the energies of the psychic world.

We live in a sea of unseen forces. My teacher, Dr. MacKie, used to say that the astral plane was the "flip side" of life in the material world. It is a world of opposites: opposites in the realm of the subjective mind, such as good and bad cravings or desires. But it's also filled with opposites in the objective psychic world as well: good and evil thought forms, entities, and subtle influences in the environment.

An example would be that even the bark of an angry dog can be very jarring to a preschooler. Dogs shoot out orange, astral projectiles from their mouths when they bark. For young children, such a psychic torpedo can pierce membranes of their consciousness.

The best word to describe a young child is "sensitive." I remember discussing this with a friend who was telepathic as a child. She said it felt like all her skin was peeled back, and she could feel the slightest breeze of a passing astral form, often in a painful way. Children are wide open to the psychic environment. Everything a caregiver does with little ones should be analyzed from the perspective of how the psychic energies might affect them.

The soft spot on an infant's head can symbolize the sensitivity of small children. The crown chakra is wide open until, in the growth process, calcification occurs, and the soft spot hardens, thus protecting the child's sensitive energy field. Similarly, when children are born, their etheric field is also loose and soft and only vaguely articulated with physical functions. Thus, psychic impacts from the outside environment can "leak" into their awareness. Later, the roots of sanskaric fibers locked in the bony structure branch out into the etheric to help solidify (relatively speaking) the child's new etheric membrane. At this stage of development, other etheric functions connected with memory and intellect effectively block out many psychic impulses.

As I write this, it is the Christmas season, and my mind goes out to all the unhappy infants being wheeled in their strollers through stores and malls. In the chapter on the environment, I described what my teacher, Murshida Duce, termed the "astral wash." Energies and thought forms generated by frantic shopping, negative moods, or anxiety take shape in astral matter. Heavy, dense, negative energies sink close to the ground and accumulate. Lighter, more pleasant forms of love or, let's say, a Christmas song you may be humming, rise up to the heart and head. I mentioned earlier that the heavy, astral "dirt" collects on your shoes, and that is the origin of religious practices of removing shoes in a temple or mosque.

Anyway, what happens to sensitive, open little children? We put them in a stroller and scoot them right through this sludge. The older baby buggies were much more civilized from the energy standpoint—lifting young children up another two feet. One can easily imagine why children get so fussy and whiny in large shopping malls. Covering the child's head can be of some help. I remember I used to cover my infant son's head with a silk hat, since silk is the best fabric to shield a child's body (and especially his crown chakra) from unpleasant astral forces. And a baby sling or backpack are great innovations. Not only do they lift small children up and out of the astral wash, they also bask in their parent's own loving energy field.

The next topic may be very unpopular with many parents. When I explain this to folks, most just ignore my recommendation. This has to do with small children and airplanes. Children are best served by not taking them on airplanes during their first year of life, at least. I learned about this from an anthroposophical doctor, Dr. Robert Gorter, from Holland. The loose etheric body of a baby is connected to the physical largely through the heart area. When you travel with the physical body going at high speeds, the lighter, more diaphanous etheric field does not follow along as fast. You can demonstrate this for yourself by riding on a roller coaster. That funny feeling of your insides "lifting" is the etheric membrane failing to keep up with the speeding physical body. Anyway, in an airplane, the etheric field is pulled along behind the physical like a flapping flag, and the sensation is not a happy one for sensitive infants. Who of us has not heard the uncontrollable crying of a baby on an airplane? Allopathic doctors explain it has to do with pain in the baby's ears from the altitude. I can assure you, the etheric discomfort is worse. Also, as the etheric field pulls away from the body, it stresses the heart connections. In fact, such etheric heart ripping, I'm told, can result in physical heart problems later in life.

"But how will we see Grandma and Grandpa if we can't fly on a plane?" I would suggest that the old folks can come to you to see the new baby. Or you could arrange to take a train. Analyzing every situation concerning young children from the perspective of unseen energies and forces doesn't always make the life of a caregiver easier.

Another topic is nature. The more you and your child can be outdoors and in nature, the better. Flowers, trees, and grass hold spiritual forces that nurture a child. And many children can clairvoyantly delight in the unseen elements in a garden, forest, river, or park.

I was talking to a child who was walking on the beach on the shore of Lake Michigan. He mentioned offhandedly, "Sometimes when I'm outside, it feels like I'm inside." What that sentence conveyed to me was that that little boy felt the nurturing, protective energies of Mother Earth embracing him in the same way he felt cozy and protected in his bedroom at home. That is the goal: to help these newly reincarnated wanderers feel comfortable and safe in their new bodies on earth.

The pollution, traffic, and noises of a city are also mirrored by the congestion of astral currents and thought forms coming at you from every which way. And small children are affected. Does that mean you shouldn't go to museums or restaurants in the city with little ones? Of course not. You simply must be continually mindful. The child's positive energy can't always fend off environmental impacts. That's why the wise parents bring a healthful, energizing snack along on excursions.

There are lots of places of questionable energy that you can easily avoid. An extreme example would be, say, to take a small child to Las Vegas. The greed and money desires are definitely an unsuitable environment for kids. I wouldn't even take a youngster into a butcher shop, as many entities are attracted by the energies of animal blood. Bars, taverns, or any place you know drugs are being used should be avoided. Remember the astral octopus Tim Leary created at his retreat in upstate New York? Now, imagine your three-year-old with superphysical tentacles around him. My wife, Hana, has strong memories of being taken to bars as a young girl. Her father was a well-known country musician, and his band often played in bars. If it was his turn to babysit his daughter, he would simply bring her with him. Hana remembers from age five or so the creepy, viscous energy she felt the moment she stepped into a bar. Her inner self wanted to flee, but her father was already at the bar with a drink in his hand.

I remember a similar incident with Blake. He was eleven, and we were overseas, visiting a famous Kali temple just outside Kathmandu, Nepal. It was a festival day, and people were lined up with goats, sheep, and chickens to be sacrificed in the temple. We, of course, being Westerners, were not welcomed near the temple. But there was a small river of animal blood flowing down the pathway near our feet, and I noticed the psychic atmosphere getting more thick and toxic. I looked at my son. His face was pale and drawn. His eyes were bleary and sleepy looking. In short, he looked ill.

"Dad," he said, "get me out of here." His etheric web could not protect him from the horrendous psychic pollution caused by animal sacrifice.

Just as you wouldn't allow a child into an active battlefield, caregivers have to shield children from astral battlefields. There are negative forces. There are negative entities. If you find yourself in a negative place, as I did in Nepal, just leave. And you need to listen to what children say. I remember Sonya, a good friend of mine, was clairvoyant as a child. She would see nasty elementals at night and be frightened. But her mother just said, "You had a nightmare; there's nothing to be afraid of. It's probably something you ate." That kind of comment makes children doubt their own perceptions or lose trust in their caregiver. I always recommend to parents that they tell a child with night fears, "Don't worry, nothing can hurt you. I'm here to protect you." Or you can say, "Your angel [or God or Jesus, etc.] will protect you."

I remember when I was a camp counselor near Philadelphia in the 1970s. It was my night for bunk duty. The children were asleep. Suddenly, Johnny started calling out and making strange sounds. I went to his bed and tried to wake him. He just kept thrashing around and making small cries. Finally, when I couldn't wake him up, I put one hand on his head and one hand on his heart, and yelled, "In the name of Meher Baba, all spirits depart!"

In the twinkling of an eye, Johnny took a deep breath and stopped jerking around. He never woke up but slept peacefully the rest of the night. So there I was, a twenty-one-year-old exorcist. Never be hesitant about countering negative energy with positive energy. With small children, subjective psychological states, tantrums, or uncontrolled crying can be strongly related to objective psychic harassment.

Phoebe Bendit, a theosophical psychic, explains the openness of children this way: "[T]he etheric field of every child is for some years entirely open and hence vulnerable to the atmosphere in which it has to live" (*The Etheric Body of Man,* 1977, p 50).

Sanskaras, the coded units of past impressions, have several layers. The etheric and astral layers of sanskaras are not really released to awaken a subjective life in the child until the age of six or seven. Dr. Rudolf Steiner, the originator of Waldorf education, goes so far as to say the etheric body isn't really "born" until age seven. What that means is that the energies of the etheric level, before age seven, are channeled into the rapid growth of the physical form. The small child is functioning with an inherited mindset. At age seven, the etheric articulates and tightens around the physical, especially in the head area; etheric sanskaras are released for expression. A subjective mentality awakens. The forces of memory awaken, and the personality from within begins to clearly assert itself.

For decades, psychologists have noticed this shift in consciousness of children. Hindu philosophers say that children don't reap the results of past-life karma or create new karma until after age seven. Psychologists, such as Jean Piaget, say children don't start to think logically until this inner change occurs.

In my years as a schoolteacher, I always felt it was terribly important to track the inner, mental changes of my kindergartners and first graders. Since I could not watch the changes in the child's etheric field of energy, I tested the students with the Piaget tasks that demonstrate whether they are thinking logically or are still in the preoperational stage. Teachers should have different expectations of children whose etheric mentality is not yet released. For example, children should not be expected to learn to read until after this intrapsychic shift occurs. They often cannot mentally remember and coordinate the quantities of variables in combining twenty-six letters with many more individual phonetic sounds into words. In Waldorf schools, reading instruction doesn't even begin until first grade. Public school standards, even the new Common Core, require kindergartners to learn to read. Rather than honoring developmental research, modern educators are "racing to the top." They think an earlier academic start will give the kids a head start. This is just another example of how a working knowledge of inner, occult, or hidden energies can have an important impact on your life and work.

If the early teaching of reading is a negative approach to education, one positive approach for elementary age children is to provide them with a steady diet of world fairy tales. These stories depict in image form the transformational and growth forces of the astral and etheric realm. Many depict the child's incarnating process into the dangerous world of materialistic reality. And after a period of trials, the hero usually finds and unites with the inner radiance of his spiritual self. He marries the princess and lives happily ever after. When caregivers tell seven-year-olds a true fairy tale, the children feel their inner being is acknowledged and the trials they face in life are understood. This topic is beyond the reach of this present volume, but I would like to share one little tidbit that might help in understanding the spiritual meaning of fairy tales.

Every character in a fairy tale (as in a dream) represents an inner aspect of the child's personality. All action in the story takes place within. With this insight, you can begin to interpret the real meaning of a tale and how it might affect a child. When Hansel and Gretel get lost in the woods, they enter a candy house ruled by a witch. This is an inner picture of the male/female soul incarnating in the appealing-looking physical body, only to find that it's ruled by the forces of materialism (the witch).

I think with education, more than in other fields I have discussed, the connection between objective, occult energies and subjective, psychological states of mind becomes most clear. When the etheric body of a child goes through the tightening around the physical body, two things happen.

First, the subjective world of children opens up to vast new realms of thinking and feeling, due to the release of a flood of sanskaric propensities. Now they don't want to be police officers or firefighters; they want to be astronomers or writers. Impressions from their own past lives are released.

Second, this new subjective mentality blocks off the former sensitivity to currents in the etheric atmosphere. Psychic children often lose their openness. Children who used to have visions of past lives now only think the thoughts from their present life. Many authors have written that children should be encouraged to keep their psychic gifts and sensitivity to astral forces. But in my view, natural developmental processes thankfully block off these distracting psychic visions.

However, during adolescence, developmental changes release new energies to the child. The striking developmental changes at puberty are in many ways far more obvious than the subtler transformation of a child at seven. How can we understand the search for identity and the tremendous shifting of thinking, feeling, and physical processes from a spiritual view?

A new level of mind is activated in an adolescent that awakens the personality for a particular lifetime, and this awakening has to do with the astral body. Previously, the etheric field had tightened and articulated with physical nervous and brain activity. Similarly, at puberty, astral forces not previously able to integrate with physical life electrify the entire body, particularly the hormonal system. As previously discussed, the astral membrane holds the energies of the personality with all its opposite traits of weakness or strength, happiness or depression, knowledge or ignorance. At puberty, this astrality is "born" and closes around the physical form, creating an ovoid membrane containing a personal crust on the astral level. This personal egg can be seen by clairvoyants and is called the aura. Intense emotions, intrinsic thoughts, and intense physical sensations are all awakened by the astral currents of life. Adolescents begin a search for self now, since before this age, they had not been as fully in touch with their core personality.

With their personality now awakened in subconscious levels on the astral plane, that egg-shaped membrane is now fully functional. If a propensity exists, a youth can suddenly become psychic, have intense astral nightmares, or be in touch with astral energies of all kinds. Remember the telepath, Linda, who would inwardly cringe to be in the presence of the chaotic astral forces of teenage boys? Teens are also often big fans of horror movies. They not only relish the intense emotions of a good scare, but they inwardly recognize the reality of astral forces related to spooks or demons. Of course, drug use at this age, though a real temptation, is disastrous. Marijuana, for instance, can blow open the tissue of the astral membrane and leave teens more vulnerable than they already are to astral impressions of greed, lust, and anger. A temper tantrum of a teen is a volcanic eruption of astral lava.

I was recently discussing teenagers with a friend of mine who was a counselor of troubled teens in a public high school. He confirmed everything we've been discussing. One of his clients is interested in spooks and asks whether ghosts are real. Another one experienced a death in the family and wanted to understand what happens after death. Still another is trying to learn how to have out-of-body experiences. And a final client talked about killing himself. My friend and he had a fascinating session discussing how one seriously interrupts one's karma when one commits suicide.

Dr. Steiner explained that this newly felt astrality affects boys differently than girls. Boys become mostly withdrawn and inward as they balance the new personality forces of their membrane. My own son became very quiet and uncommunicative during his first year after puberty. I was worried because I was a single father, and Blake and I had always enjoyed an easy, flowing communication. I decided to take a course on adolescence at the Rudolf Steiner College in Fair Oaks, California. I described my son's behavior to the instructor, Betty Staley, and she laughed and laughed.

"It's very common for teenage boys to be uncommunicative and withdrawn," Staley said. "All their mental and emotional energy is being taken up integrating the new astral sheath. I've always felt boys should wear a sign around their necks, saying, 'Closed for Reconstruction.'" This new understanding really helped me and gave me an insight into his subconscious. And as I relaxed around him, Blake could feel free to go through his inner "reconstruction" processes.

If boys focus their energies inwardly, Steiner said that girls are the opposite. They become focused outwardly into socializing. It's a familiar image to see teenage girls on the phone all the time or discussing anything and everything at parties. This kind of outward-oriented behavior assists them in channeling their new growth forces. Of course, these forces can be easily misdirected or distorted. Then you find conditions like anorexia or bulimia in teen girls.

In fact, in anthroposophical medicine, it's been stated that if the astral body is wrongly integrated with the physical organism during adolescence, it can become the cause of future illness. And it's true that teens can be vulnerable to special illnesses like infectious mononucleosis.

One final warning for teenagers would be to not dabble with ritualistic magic, hypnotism, mediumship, or Ouija boards. Because of their openness to astral realms, if they call on a spirit, it might just come.

A good friend of mine related to me her teenage adventures with a very nasty, dark entity. She and her best friend started playing with the Ouija board. Leaving their auras open, while also transmitting the ever-present adolescent excitement tinged with sexual energy, they easily attracted an invisible entity. Once called, the astral spook was not easy to banish. It would give messages to my friend through the other girl's mouth. The other girl would write letters in which the entity communicated. And my friend was even sexually molested by this unseen presence.

Here's how the episode ended: My friend heard about the master Meher Baba, and she went to a meeting led by Darwin Shaw, a longtime devotee. After the meeting, Darwin gave her a small button with Baba's photo. "This button has been touched by Baba," Darwin announced. Instinctively, my friend lifted the button to her forehead. "Immediately," she told me, "I felt an opening in the back of my head click shut."

That open center or chakra allowed the entity into her consciousness. Once it shut, she had no more psychic difficulties. But even after forty-five years, her friend who channeled the entity is still bothered by unpleasant astral forces.

This reminds me of another Meher Baba story I related in *The Secret Life of Kids.* My friend Charmian was a very open psychic child. Her psychic abilities did not close down as she grew up. Even into her college years, Charmian saw spooks, saw auras, and could hear people's thoughts. In 1948, she and her mother went to India to see Meher Baba. One of the first things Baba did was to hold Charmian's wrist and say, "I want you to live in one world at a time." Charmian told me it was like he turned off a faucet. All her psychic abilities were instantly shut off and blocked.

The next topic is not something I know anything about but it is speculation. In parapsychological research, when scientists are looking for psychic activity, a ghostly presence, or poltergeists, they often use electromagnetic radiation (EMR) meters. It seems that psychic episodes are connected with a spike in EMR. Adolescents are not only intrigued with ghosts, but they also surround themselves with a continual human-made forcefield of electromagnetic radiation through their cell phones, computers, and musical devices. In fact, a scientist told me that the part of the brain associated with addictions is strongly activated when teens use their wireless devices. Many teens check their emails or Facebook page many times an hour on their smart phones. *Time* magazine has reported that late teens and college students use electronic devices six to eight hours a day.

I already discussed the health risks of overexposure to the energies of EMR in the technology chapter. But here, I'm just posing the questions as to whether human-made EMR might be connected to the astral EMR of spooks. Might teens be getting some astral stimulation from mobile devices?

Understanding and honoring the inner forces that gradually awaken and exert their specific influences with a developing child is obviously a complex issue. Psychologists can spend a lifetime seeking to understand developmental processes without even taking unseen forces into account. An incarnate child is sort of like an iceberg; the part floating above water is only a small fraction of the entire formation. Understanding the invisible, hidden layers of a child's mentality seems crucial in honoring the true child.

When the astral membrane is fully integrated and the personal identity is provisionally established, the young person between the ages of eighteen and twenty-one is ready to go out into the world. As Meher Baba's sister told me, they are ready to pick up where they left off in their last life. So more, and final, changes can be noticed in a twenty-year-old's personality. An example that illustrates this new shift in consciousness is a story concerning John, my best friend in high school. John and I joined the Theosophical Society together. He was very interested in astral projection. After my first semester at UC Berkeley, I bought John a copy of the theosophical textbook *The Secret Doctrine* as a very special gift for Christmas.

When I proudly presented my gift, John said with a smirk, "Good heavens, Jim, are you still into that stuff?" His personality had gone through a transition, and the astral plane of his teen years no longer interested him.

So at this point in life, you pick up your adult sanskaras and move forward. In my own case, I always thought I wanted to follow in my father's footsteps and become a doctor. But at age twenty-one, I discovered I wanted to work with children. In fact, I had no interest or ability in science at all.

Of course, in this chapter, I haven't really discussed actual techniques or methods of education or child-rearing. Rather, I have focused on the hidden side of life and the inner currents and energies of children's subjective experiences and how they cope with these currents as they grow up. An understanding of the spiritual side of child development is crucial for a caregiver to understand in this coming new age. Such knowledge enlivens everything you do with children. In teaching a child a fairy tale, for example, Dr. Steiner said that it's important for the storyteller to mentally understand the images of the story and what they mean for inner development. You don't communicate such thoughts to the child, of course, but an interpretation of the meaning of the story adds tremendous energy to the tale when it's transmitted. Children feel it's a truly significant message for them, worth remembering. In a similar way, an inner awareness of the unseen energies working through children helps bring living consciousness to every thought, word, and deed in your activities with children.

CHAPTER 14

The Dead

The most dynamic and ubiquitous of all unseen occult forces, of course, are generated by human beings. We are dynamos of all sorts of etheric currents, related to mind and heart and simply the energies that keep the physical body going. The human energy field is powerful. We can truly gauge the incredible energies we normally channel when healthy.

If you've ever seen a corpse, the tremendous impression is that here is a shell with no shred of life energy. But spiritual wisdom that has been transmitted to students down through the eons attest to the fact that human energies do not dissipate at the time of death. People do not change at death; they merely shift their level of consciousness and take off the physical code that was their mortal body. So if the energies of live people interest and affect us constantly, then the dead must be reckoned with as well.

I'd like to begin this chapter with my favorite story about dead people. It isn't exactly relevant to the type of inner energies we've been discussing. But then, this is my book, and I can write anything I want to. It's an anecdote from a little book called *Letters from a Living Dead Man,* which was written around 1914. There was this old judge in Los Angeles who, when he passed away, wanted to transmit to someone still alive a little bit about what the inner worlds were like or, as the Egyptians would say, a little bit about the Land of the Dead.

The letters were transmitted to a woman named Elza Harker, at the time living in Paris. They were transmitted through the process of automatic writing. This type of writing isn't something I'd recommend dabbling in, but nevertheless, there have been some interesting tracks written through this technique down through the years.

Anyway, our judge was being guided through one of the areas of the astral plane by an invisible helper he met after death. They came upon a man curled up in a ball, in a comatose state.

The judge inquired, "What's wrong with that man?"

"Oh," the guide answered, "in life, that fellow was a staunch atheist and believed that there was no afterlife, only oblivion. So that's what he's experiencing: his own extinction of consciousness."

"Can we help him?" the judge asked. "Can we wake him up to his after-death consciousness?"

"Go ahead, try."

The judge prodded the figure, shook him, yelled at him, but got no response.

The guide said, "Sometimes people remain in this void state for up to a hundred years. With luck, he'll slowly wake up after a while."

Meher Baba once said, "Life after death is every bit as much of a certainty as death after life." Nowadays, the medically facilitated "near-death experience," reported by thousands of people, proves to every rational, objective mind that there is consciousness after death and that consciousness is not dependent on the brain or other bodily processes. Knowing that there is nothing to be afraid of after death is common among spiritual students. However, there are aspects of death and the residual energies of dead people that can and do affect us on earth. And some of these energies can be a bit scary.

There are two factors that generally make interaction with dead people rare. The first is the etheric web, which we discussed in several chapters. The etheric chakras are like conduits for impressions from the inner realms of mental and emotional energies. But there exist screens over the chakras that do not allow objective, psychic impulses to seep into consciousness. Energies of the dead would have to somehow bridge the gulf to be registered in someone's consciousness. Drug addicts, alcoholics, or others impair the etheric web and are more likely to have interactions with the dead, as well as psychics or mediums who have rich mechanisms that allow communications between realms.

The second factor is that dead people rarely remain close enough to the earth plane to have interactions with incarnate people. Usually, within a matter of hours or at the most days, they are swept by astral currents to higher areas of heaven to get on with the personal tasks that need to be accomplished. Sometimes, newly deceased people inform a close relative or friend that they have died, just before leaving the energy field of the earth's aura. I wrote about one such case in *The Secret Life of Kids*:

> [Charmian] was eight at the time and was lying down for a nap when a "lovely lady appeared by my bed. She had violet eyes and long, brown curls in her hair. She smiled sweetly at me." Charmian had never seen the woman before, and though she seemed completely solid and normal and "real," the experience frightened the little girl, who called for her mother. The lady began fading away, disintegrating in patches, much like a cloud of smoke. By the time the mother arrived in the bedroom, the lady had vanished. Charmian explained to her mother what had happened and tried to describe the lovely visitor. The description seemed familiar to the girl's mother, and she showed Charmian five or six photos. Charmian was able to identify the woman as the subject of one of the photos. This was a friend of the mother, named Nell Peterson.
>
> About this time the doorbell rang, and a telegram was delivered. It was a message from Mr. Peterson that his wife, Nell, had died suddenly.
>
> Charmian's mother then understood. "Nell always wanted to meet you," she told her daughter. "I guess now she has." (pp 112–13)

I also had a happy experience when my mom died. My mother passed away at age eighty-four from a heart attack. My three brothers and I rented a boat in Florida to scatter her ashes at sea, as she had requested. As we each threw handfuls of ashes in the ocean, the ashes came together and formed a lovely turquoise cloud-like shape in the water, almost like a giant blue jellyfish. Then I saw, in my mind's eye, a clear image of my mother, in a young twentysomething body, flying over the sea around our ship with a huge smile on her face. I felt a definite confirmation that she was there with us and so very happy to be relieved of her old, crippled physical body.

It's quite common for deceased people to join loved ones after death and often attend their own funeral. They often try to console relatives and attempt to contact them—at least through thoughts—and communicate that they're still here, still "alive," and not to be sad. In fact, many spiritual teachers and counselors recommend not being sad at funerals in order to assist the dead to move on. Excessive grief inclines the dead to stay in the earth energy field to try to console friends and relatives.

At my grandmother's funeral, I made a giant card and drew a ship departing over the ocean, with the message "Bon voyage, Grandma." I had all her friends sign the card. It was a nice way for everyone to affirm her new phase of existence or, as Murshid MacKie used to say, the flip side of life.

Of course, cheeriness at a funeral can offend some people. My father's memorial was an example. My first spiritual teacher, Murshida Ivy Duce, used to tell her students to try to be cheerful and not overly sad at funerals. It helps the dead move on. And, she said, the departed person will most certainly be there with you at the funeral. In 1971, my father drowned while on vacation in Hawaii. The body was never recovered, but a lifeguard had spotted him well out in the water. He was officially listed as missing for seven years. But the family members knew he had died.

All the family gathered at our Wilmette, Illinois, home for a memorial. My teacher in San Francisco admonished me to try to be cheerful, for my father's sake. Well, I was cheerful—too cheerful. For my seventeen-year-old brother, Rick, I set a striking example as to how to deal with the death of a dear family member. With the rest of the family, however, my cheeriness was seen as cold, aloof, and without feelings. They very much resented my cheerful attitude. Obviously, you have to use your intuition and harmonize with the situation. I was too stubbornly trying to follow my teacher's advice and hurt the feelings of my family members.

But funerals in general are a good example of how the unseen presence of an astral human can affect us on the gross plane, and more importantly, how we can use our own energies of love and goodwill to communicate with and boost the energies of our loved ones on the inner planes. The conscious use of spiritual energies goes both ways.

When I was in college, I used to enjoy studying in cemeteries. I don't know; they were always so peaceful and beautiful—like a park that few people visited. It was a pattern of mine to head for a cemetery each afternoon to read or write papers. When my Sufi teacher found out that I frequented cemeteries, even taking naps there, she was strongly against the practice. "You don't know what shade could be hanging out there," she said, "having an unpleasant influence over you."

So, what is the part of the dead human who can hang out in cemeteries or a nice English castle? From my fifty years of study, I have learned there are three types of energies that can cause a typical haunting. The first involves the grayish-white mist sometimes seen over graves and floating down corridors in houses. This is called a shade. It is the residual energy from the etheric body, discarded and no longer used by the indwelling human entity. Souls that are addicted to earthly life often reanimate themselves temporarily and use an etheric shell to become visible to incarnate beings. Also, various elemental beings can reactivate a shell for a time, or it can even be electrified by a strong thought form. Such a reanimated etheric body may be the kernel of truth behind the idea of the zombie, or reanimated corpse. Such shells have little power and no real energy to help or harm incarnate people.

Another cause for hauntings is leftover, residual sanskaras, loaded with force but confined to a particular space. These are the cause of noises, footsteps, or commotion in a particular room that repeats itself, say, every Wednesday night at midnight. Some horrifying accident or crisis or suicide could have stamped its etheric force on the objects in a room and sort of replay a movie of the original incident from time to time. The energies you might see in such a haunting are like psychic videos, rather than being an actual earthbound spirit.

The third and probably rarest type of haunting is the presence of an actual, earthbound, astral membrane of a deceased human being. Humans can get stuck to the earth plane by violent accidents, crises, suicides, or addictions of various kinds—including alcohol, drugs, or even sexual addictions. They are earthbound because these entities don't want to move into higher realms or cannot make the inner transition because they enjoy the aroma of earthly experiences and experience it vicariously. These are the souls popularized in trendy television shows and movies when the medium assists an astral traveler to go "into the light."

Many of us have had experiences of seeing or feeling some sort of presence in a particular house or location. It doesn't matter which of the preceding causes precipitated these creepy feelings. Such experiences, however, in my opinion, can have beneficial effects on the spiritual student. For one thing, a haunted house can offer proof that energies, influences, and entities that are nonphysical really exist on some subjective level of inner consciousness. When most of science tries to force materialism on the gullible public, an occasional psychic experience can offer therapeutic confirmation of the existence of nonphysical reality.

Let me offer an anecdote of my own as an illustration of such psychic experiences. My first experience of a haunted house occurred in 1976 while on a European trip with my brother and my grandmother. She was a spry kid of merely eighty-three years at the time. She had a wonderful experience as we drove through central England. By chance, we motored to the town of Epworth, the birthplace of John Wesley. My grandmother, a lifelong Methodist and widow of a minister, was thrilled by our accidental arrival in Epworth. After spending the night in a tavern where Wesley had stayed, the next day we had an interesting tour of the Wesley family home. On the third floor, I entered a room that felt instantly creepy with a kind of thick, viscous atmosphere. "This," the guide answered, "is Jeffrey's room. He's the Wesley family ghost." This ghost had been making infrequent appearances for 300 years, which is a giveaway that the ghostly presence is sanskaric or residual life force. However, the experience clearly demonstrated to me the feelings connected with a definite and authenticated haunting.

In 1997, my son, Blake, and I returned to the British Isles. On our way to Scotland, we decided to pop by Chillingham Castle, the subject of a TV program on ghosts that we had both seen. Chillingham was touted as being the "most haunted" site in England, though it was still inhabited by its current owners. The sections of the castle tourists have a chance to visit really did have that same creepy feeling I recognized from the experience in Jeffrey's room. When we visited the dungeon, full of medieval instruments of torture, however, the feeling was as if the ceiling was pressing down on one's consciousness. The atmosphere was incredibly oppressive, and we were about to leave when a jet overhead broke the sound barrier. The boom gave us a real "jump"!

Continuing our trip up to Scotland, we encountered a haunted bed and breakfast in Arbrouth. We had thought we were heading for a nice seaside city, but instead we found a rundown industrial port with depressing neighborhoods. We found a bed and breakfast in an old, abandoned apartment building. Always one to save a few dollars, I should have paid attention to the room and not all the pounds I was saving. The second-floor room had a cheery window, but the bed was broken down and the carpet was filthy. When darkness descended, Blake started seeing "ghost rats" scurrying across the floor. Ghost rats was a term he coined for "black smudges, around a foot long, that zip across the floor, floating 5 or 6 inches from the rug." And they definitely carried with them an unpleasant feeling. The atmosphere in our room got more and more oppressive. I started repeating my mantra and psychically trying to clear the space out a little. I lit a candle and a stick of incense and put them by the locked door. The bed sagged so much that we had to take the mattress off the bed frame and put it on the floor. Various creaks and groans of the old building gave us a very restless night. No doubt some folks who stayed in that room left a sanskaric residue. Or, perhaps it was the whole building. But once one recognizes that nasty psychic energy connected with hauntings, one has the impulse to flee, even though there's probably no real danger.

Sometimes hauntings don't generate that oppressive atmosphere. Once, my son and I were staying in a grand old Victorian house in Lexington, Massachusetts. One evening, Blake drew me aside and whispered, "I just saw a 7-foot-high white man with a flat head float up the hall stairway. At the top, he just vanished." The white man didn't seem to affect the psychic atmosphere of the house at all, and we had a pleasant stay there.

Can a spook really affect one's energy field or psychological wellbeing here on earth? The answer is yes, but encountering spooks is really quite rare. The dead are certainly around us. Even if one merely counts the people who have died a normal death and are around for three or four days while they acclimatize to life without a physical body, we are talking about an enormous population of spooks. Also, at any one time, the population of astral bodies of deceased people is far greater than the population of physical bodies on earth. But generally, such dead people exist on a completely different wavelength of energy than us earthly folks. It's like tuning a radio. When you dial out a news program and tune in a music station, the news is completely out of one's consciousness and cannot be detected, even though certainly the channel's electromagnetic impulse is still there. Only souls who make an effort to cling to semi-earthly consciousness can sometimes be detected. These are, as I've mentioned, victims of violent crime, suicides, or drug addicts and, in some cases, accident victims.

And some dead people don't even know they are dead. I contacted my father after he had drowned in Hawaii. I found him on the beach off which the accident had occurred. He was dressed in his tennis clothes and wanted to play a game with me. He had no idea he was dead. In fact, a spiritual counselor told me some time later that it took my father over two months to figure out that he was dead and needed to move on to the astral. He was an atheist in life and believed strongly that death simply meant oblivion. So naturally, when he found himself ready for a tennis game, he certainly couldn't be dead.

It's common knowledge that dabbling with Ouija boards can actually draw the attention of a spook—sometimes with very negative consequences. My wife told me that she and a girlfriend as teenagers used to "play" with a Ouija board, and when spooks were attracted, Hana could actually see them. She particularly saw them when she and her girlfriend played down by some railroad tracks near a gully. But why are these unpleasant influences from the astral attracted by Ouija boards or in other ways? The *Tibetan Book of the Dead* discusses "hungry ghosts." These ghosts are basically deceased humans who are very attached to some aspect of earthly life, and they are unable to transcend these desires. Because they are unable to express their emotions through a physical body, they emanate unpleasant psychic energies. Perhaps it was this type of energy that Blake and I felt in that haunted bed and breakfast in Scotland.

Then there is the topic of possession. The cases of true spirit-possession are thankfully rare, but I have come across some examples. Some deceased people are caught in a limbo state between the astral and physical worlds. These people sometimes prey on incarnate people's energy, either to express their frustrated desires or to garner enough psychic force to propel them into the next spiritual realm.

Drug users, alcoholics, and ill people with high fevers can often have loose or damaged etheric webs and can let influences from the "hungry ghosts" obsess them or even possess them. It seems clear to me that some folks who wind up in mental hospitals often are being plagued by such outside entities.

Unfortunately, children can be susceptible as well. As I discussed in my education chapter, children go through significant psychic transitional states between the ages of five and seven and again in puberty. A traumatic event during either of these transitional phases can unbalance a child's psyche and leave him temporarily open to possession.

The two cases I am personally familiar with I discussed in my book, *The Secret Life of Kids.* The first child was possessed after a high fever, and the second was overshadowed after a traumatic blow to the head. I might as well simply quote from my earlier work:

> Five years ago Timmy seemed normal enough. He was affectionate and bright and had high-powered, professional parents. One day Timmy became ill, with an extremely high fever that lasted for two days. After the fever broke and Timmy recovered his health, he started behaving peculiarly. He had fits of extreme anger and violence and would scream at his parents, using the most vulgar and coarse language. These fits seemed so uncharacteristic of Timmy that his parents became worried. Over a period of several weeks the fits became more and more frequent, until his entire personality seemed to express angry vulgarity.
>
> Much of the violence seemed to be channeled toward family members. One day, following a screaming tirade, Timmy grabbed a large kitchen knife, ran to his mother with the knife held high and screamed, "Mom, kill me! Use this knife and kill me. You must! Then he collapsed.
>
> His parents sought the help of a spiritual teacher, who, in turn, discussed the case with a psychic counselor. They

determined that Timmy had, in fact, been possessed by a malevolent and extremely violent being of some sort. It was also suggested that his momentary desire to kill himself stemmed from an instinctive effort to rid himself of the psychic intruder. The parents were told to never leave Timmy alone and to offer constant support and love. In the meantime, a group of friends gathered daily to pray the entity be allowed to go its way and leave Timmy alone.

After about a week the fits stopped, and Timmy seemed gradually to return to his old self. Once Timmy's former personality reasserted itself, he had no further trouble with the paranormal intruder. He went on to lead a normal and happy childhood....Today Timmy has no recollection of the possession; he only remembers that there was a disturbing period in his childhood when everybody seemed to be very worried about him. (p 213)

I don't doubt this story at all, because Timmy became a student of mine, and I was one of the members of the prayer group. So there definitely can be scary intrusions of the energy fields of the dead into the world of the living.

Another anecdote I reported in my earlier book involves a boy I did not know. This boy, at the age of six had a bad fall, struck his head, and was knocked unconscious. When he woke up, he had become a completely different person. He would swear, have temper tantrums, and get into frequent fights with other children. This unpleasant, altered personality lasted eight years!

Finally, again at the transitional age of 14, he had another accident and was again knocked unconscious. This time, his old personality returned. This boy had full recollection of what had occurred. He said that for these eight years he had hovered over his body and watched while a nasty spook had used his vehicle. He was not able to get back into his physical body until the next accident forced the "hungry ghosts" out and the boy was able to zip back into his physical form.

Of course, possessions aren't as common as Hollywood would have us believe. However, children should be encouraged to keep in energetic, active modes of thinking and not to make their minds blank or passive. The etheric web is developing during this period from 7 to 14 and hasn't yet reached its mature functioning, which serves to filter out unwanted astral influences from consciousness. That's one of the worries spiritually conscious people have about legalizing marijuana. If pot gets into the hands of children, it can really open the doors to psychic mischief makers.

Adolescence is a period when a child is opening and adjusting to the astral membrane of his mind. Because they are connecting with the astral world, teens often go through a period when they are fascinated by books or movies on occult subjects. Drugs, Ouija boards, magical rituals can be effective ways of invoking deceased people who are stuck in an emotional limbo state. Healthy, sweet, well-adjusted people move into higher realms when they die, as they are meant to do. It's primarily maladjusted, nasty spirits who are the ones available to eager, experimenting teens.

A footnote to this discussion involves the spiritual master, Meher Baba. Often, close companions of Meher Baba would hear and see things at various places where Baba stayed during nights while traveling. One of Meher Baba's close ones was once on night watch. Peering into the darkness, Arjun saw two gigantic white human forms. As he watched them, they became larger and more ominous. They reached almost 20 feet in height. He was petrified and could not utter a sound. Just then, Meher Baba emerged from his room. Arjun gestured to the darkness, but the spooks had disappeared. Baba said, "Didn't I tell you not to be afraid when I am here? Those were ghosts who came to me, seeking rebirth. Such spirits of the dead have committed suicide and are unable to take another birth for several centuries. Every night such ghosts come to me; so never be afraid. They won't harm you." (*Lord Meher,* p 283)

One can easily surmise from our discussions that professional mediums, spiritualists, and even channelers who purposefully contact astral spooks are often not contacting well-adjusted deceased spirits. Trying to help the dead who are in trouble, like the well-known medium Allison DuBois, can be a form of selfless service. Contacting the dead to appease the curiosity of living relatives or to get messages of spiritual wisdom, in my opinion, is not productive or helpful for anyone. As I have read in so many books, just because a person is dead doesn't make him wise or any kind of a spiritual authority. A mobster still has the criminal mind of a mobster, whether dead or alive.

The population of the dead hovering in the astral field of the earth is always far greater than the population of physical bodies on earth. In addition, the astral is home to many elementals, angels, invisible helpers, and spirit animals. It is also home to an array of unhelpful entities working against the tide of divine evolution. The energy fields of many beings can and do affect us. Sri Aurobindo, the great master of South India, spoke at length about his spiritual work during World War II. He said that Hitler had enlisted the help of countless evil entities to assist him in his creation of the Third Reich. These demonic beings Aurobindo referred to as *asuras*. Fortunately, the spiritual hierarchy blocked these asuras from fulfilling the dream of Hitler.

In conclusion, I will repeat: The dead are around us, but one doesn't have to worry about them peeking at you in the bathroom. They have better things to do, and they have a beautifully colorful and magical realm to explore. There are, however, such things as earthbound spirits and the unpleasant residue that one can come across in various localities. And it's also true that astral shells can be found reenacting horrific events in old manor houses and elsewhere. But the spirit world should not be feared. None of its inhabitants can hurt us. We are protected and blocked from such influences. And if we ever feel threatened or scared of unseen influences, we can always call on the masters, or angels, or go right to the top and call on the omnipotent God, and we will find aid and comfort from psychic distress. If a fearful entity is encountered, in 90% of the cases, as Jesus said, "he knows not what he does." Just bless him and send him on his way.

CHAPTER 15

The Human Being

This entire book is about how people can become more sensitive to the subtle currents of energy always around them and learn to observe their effects in every aspect of daily life. It hardly seems necessary to include a discussion of the human being, because this book is completely *about* human beings.

There are, though, some considerations that must be separately analyzed. All processes in the body, such as brain and nervous activity, generate an electromagnetic field radiating out. The interpenetrating astral and etheric fields, however, form the occult basis for the detection of our most important energy systems. This energy structure can be seen by some as emanating from a person and is called the aura. The so-called "health aura" is formed from the outer membrane of the etheric formative forces surrounding each of us, while the astral egg denotes changing emotional and mental energies whipping through our personality.

During the 1990s, I had an interesting experience while teaching my students. I was totally exhausted one day and was sitting for a moment in my rocking chair, trying to breathe in some energy. A six-year-old student named Noah walked by me. He said the "lines of power" that usually come straight out of my body were seriously drooping down to the floor. He was seeing etheric radiations of the health aura, because the next day, I came down with a severe cold.

There are many books that describe how the energy and color of an aura change according to moods, emotions, and types of thinking. My research into clairvoyant children started in 1969 when a couple of six-year-old boys noticed my distinctive aura while I was meditating. Information can be studied by reading books such as *The Personal Aura* by Dora Kunz.

Another concept relating to this subtle human energy field is the Chinese concept of meridians of chi running through the body. This system provides a framework for working with etheric currents in medicine. In my studies, I learned that the etheric membrane holds the roots of sanskaric threads that condition the energy of the body. Sanskaric fibers hold the coded energies from past conditioning that link the physical system to conditioned thoughts, feelings, and desires from the inner being. Psychologists talk about conditioned patterns of behavior locked in the brain and nervous functions. Of course, conditioning can be on various levels. If a mother was a drug addict during pregnancy, the conditioning in a baby's physical body may lead to weakened health later in life.

The theory of sanskaras, however, includes primarily conditioning from previous lifetimes. Sanskaras consolidate and mold the tissue of a physical body. The energy that is released when sanskaras are expressed literally drives a person into physical behavior patterns. For example, many of my friends look forward to Super Bowl Sunday. They gather around the TV and release tremendous astral energies by yelling and screaming and jumping up and down while watching the game. I have no sanskaras that connect me to any spectator sport, so I watch these friends and am astonished at their response to sports teams. They are due to sanskaras. So just imagine the billions and trillions of sanskaras we have embedded in our tissues. The theory of sanskaras constitutes a different way of understanding energies that make up our human consciousness.

And then there is karma. Karma is related to sanskaras but is really a different matter altogether. You can't discuss the energy structure of human beings without understanding sanskaras. Sanskaras are those units of mind-stuff coded with the energy of every thought, word, or deed from the past. These impressions crave the expenditure of their energies by recreating the activities that initially created them. When sanskaras bind human beings together, it's called karma, which means "action" in Sanskrit. Physics tells us when there is an action, the universal law creates an equal and opposite reaction. The universe tries to maintain balance by moving between opposing forces. So, in my personal opinion, when you have karma with someone, it means there is an imbalance that strives to return to an equilibrium point.

Here's an example of sanskaras versus karma. Let's say you are in school and love to study books, ideas, and philosophy. This is the result of sanskaras from the past and will result in, perhaps, intellectual or academic pursuits in future lives.

But now, let's say this intellectual bent has gone to your head. You brag about your insights and use your brilliance to put others down. Perhaps your relationship with your brother is based on your feeling of superiority, and you continually try to prove that he is simpleminded and can't hold a candle to your brilliance. Your brother comes to resent you. Here is a karma being created. The unbalanced energy generated between two people will persist in mental realms until the two of you balance out your sanskaras at some point in the future. Sanskaras are always connected with karma, but sanskaric tendencies do not always imply karma. Everything is not karma, but everything is sanskaras and the energy forces bound in sanskaras.

In this example, you judge others as stupid compared to your superior intellect. Perhaps in a future life, you might balance this tendency by being born with a developmental disability and your former brother is your caregiver. Energies within human beings seek to find equilibrium, balance.

Now we come to another frequently misunderstood topic: the chakras. Part of the structure of the subtle and the etheric anatomy involves energy vortexes called chakras, a Sanskrit word meaning "wheel." A vortex in the earth is where earth currents throb and pulsate into the outer environment. A chakra in the human system similarly is a connecting point where the etheric, vital body resonates and joins with the inner psycho-spiritual self. I think of them as kind of like plugs or outlets of psychic electricity. There are forty-nine major chakras, but seven are usually considered the most central. I have heard them described as cups, wheels, flowers, centers, and whirlpools; my own teacher describes them as globes or spheres. For most of us, the chakras function to channel mental, emotional, and vital forces into the circulatory system on the etheric level. Some systems of medical therapy focus on the chakras, such as polarity therapy. And some meditation practices strive to concentrate on and open the chakras, such as Tantric yoga. It is said that by opening the chakras, you can activate the seven psychic senses.

However, according to my personal spiritual study and in my own humble opinion, I believe the chakras should be left alone to do their natural work of transmitting energies from the inner planes to the physical systems. It's like yogis who learn to control their heartbeats or breath. These systems work fine on their own, and putting psychic energy into controlling such processes seems a waste of vital force.

However, at certain times, I do believe the chakras become electrified and stimulated by the shakti force at the base of the etheric spine. This latent force is called kundalini. I will only outline a teaching here, because I don't know exactly how it works from remembered personal experiences. Kundalini does not just ascend the spine once, developing or opening spiritual powers. According to the principles I have studied, human beings devote a certain series of incarnations to the mastery of very specific life lessons. For example, let's say, one such life lesson would be to become a perfect caregiver for children. In this series of lives, you may have been the head of an orphanage, a teacher, and single parent of numerous children. After you have mastered those lessons, there comes a point when working with children is no longer relevant for your soul's growth. As I understand the process, sanskaras connected with the mastery of a specific life goal are then lifted and released, burned away, or unwound. As sanskaras unwind, they stimulate the force of kundalini to lift them up through the chakras, electrifying these centers temporarily. The movement of that process in this age is up the front of the body. As my Murshid used to say, "Now, in this new age, channeling the forces through the spine is 'backward.'"

So as this set of sanskaras ascends through the chakras, the outer layer of the fibers burn away, and what is left is that inner core of light that continues to ascend through the head and eventually connects with the superphysical structure of the higher part of the mind. My teacher called this light, "molten, electrified, accelerated light." The new inner connections create spiritual light that floods the physico-etheric system, and with this light comes the beginning flow of a higher mental force: the (consciousness) flow of intuition and inspiration.

Once all these new illuminating forces are balanced and equilibrated, the kundalini withdraws again to its hiding place, and a new path of learning is explored by the person in numerous lifetimes. It should be noted that this release of sanskaric energies from a specific type of learning can take more than one life to complete; the physical body will likely be affected by the released forces. These spiritual processes are not necessarily pain-free.

This teaching appeals to me because it depicts a recurring process of gradual, spiraling, spiritual growth. If the kundalini force abides in human beings, it's logical it would not just be used as a one-shot unfolding of yogic enlightenment but would contribute to many facets of spiritual growth and illumination.

Another important point to remember is that these processes of burning away conditioned impressions of past learning can only take place when you are incarnate in a physical body. Indeed, even the cells of the body are altered by these forceful processes. As the Mother of the Sri Aurobindo ashram stated, "Expect nothing from death, life is your salvation. It is in life that you must transform yourself. It is on earth that you progress and on earth that you realize. It is in the body that you win the victory." The light released in spiritual growth can only occur through living in the physical world.

Meher Baba describes what is called the "spiritual path" as the process of gradually unwinding the conditioning of the mind, which consists of sanskaras. As sanskaras are unwound, spiritual force is released, and the individual experiences an expansion of consciousness. Eventually the unclouding of the mind gives rise to the experience of the first plane of consciousness of the subtle world.

This has nothing to do with developing psychic senses. Obviously, if first-plane consciousness results from the unwinding or unveiling of the mind, it is a permanent state; it doesn't come and go. Psychic experiences can be a byproduct of spiritual unfoldment, but the processes involved in spiritual growth are quite different. I like to conceive of it in this way: Having a psychic sense developed is like looking through a window into a beautiful mansion. The sights and sounds are unimaginably transforming. However, the unfoldment of higher consciousness through the deconditioning of the mind is like actually entering the mansion and living in the rooms. And, as the Bible tells us, "In my father's house are many mansions." The sights and sounds seen by a psychic are similar to those seen by a person with advanced consciousness. But the state of mind differs immeasurably. Imagine the difference between being out in a snowstorm, looking through a window into a warm, cozy room from the outside. You can barely hear the conversations within and cannot feel the heat from the blazing fireplace at all. What a different experience the owner of the house has, snuggling on a comfortable couch, reading a detective novel, and feeling the warming glow of the fire.

The inner light-energy available to human beings might take them toward psychic unfolding or toward unwinding spiritual processes. In my opinion, working on enlivening psychic experiences seems a relative waste of time. However, most of the topics included in this book assume you have, to a certain degree, a sensitivity to the forces from the unseen realms. When I visited Sedona, Arizona, I meditated at the Cathedral Rock energy vortex, a powerful earth energy center. I had an amazing experience of communing with the earth through my heart chakra. I think such experiences for spiritual students are an important encouragement on the path we have chosen. Such sensitivities and experiences, in a way, are psychic. But I'm not in favor of elaborate exercises to encourage or develop psychic gifts. Most professional psychics are born with their so-called gifts. This means they have psychic skills as one of their talents carried over from past lives. Such an in-born psychic talent is balanced into one's sanskaric structure. Trying to force open psychic doorways can serve to unbalance your etheric nets and precipitate mental illness.

I would like to end this chapter on the unseen energies available in human growth and learning with some practical considerations. Some folks seem to be able to draw on almost limitless inner currents of the life force. They jump out of bed filled with energy for doing, and they hardly stop till it's time for bed at night. One friend, born in the sign of Aries, told me his whole life is "driven." He never lacks for energy. I, on the other hand, have never had that type of energy matrix. It may be because of my astrological sheath of mostly water or emotional energies (I have five planets in water). I can almost feel the pulse of life energies come and go, almost like the waves on an ocean beach. Sometimes, there will even be a huge wave that fills me with tremendous force. But such force is elusive and temporary and unpredictable.

Or my delicate energy structure may be due to physical conditions such as my inherited polycystic kidney disease. After all, in Chinese medicine, the kidneys are the root of chi, the etheric force behind physical life processes. But regardless of the source of my somewhat elusive energy, it has been a lifelong concern and challenge. So if you are experiencing a low ebb of energy, I may be able to offer some helpful suggestions. As my friend Jiddu Krishnamurti used to say, "Stay with this feeling of low energy and see what it offers and where its roots are." A deflated feeling can lead you to an inward aliveness that can awaken a nice meditative state. Of course, another way of approaching the issue is to use meditation or simply sitting quietly and breathing as a good way to revive yourself on every level.

My favorite and most reliable energy generation technique has always been a twenty-minute power nap. Since I started the regular practice of meditation fifty years ago, I have, as a happy side effect, been able to get fairly quickly into a very relaxed state in a nap. I don't need to do any formal meditative practice or use my mantra or anything. I simply lie down, close my eyes, and try not to think. My body gets profoundly still—sort of a numb feeling—and I rarely even fall asleep. After fifteen minutes or so, I can get up feeling completely refreshed. During my working years, I would always take such a power nap during my lunch break, before my afternoon class. I don't think I could have gotten through my afternoon of teaching without my etheric revival, my short nap.

Dr. Steiner used to recommend a little lie-down after a meal. He said the etheric forces of the body needed to focus on the digestive (metabolic) processes for a few minutes, away from the nerve-sense system of brain activity. What many people do to counteract the brain lethargy after a meal is to have a sugary dessert or a cup of strong coffee to activate the thinking brain. Dr. Steiner suggested a short nap would be more in harmony with bodily needs. One of my dear anthroposophical friends, the famous artist Maulsby Kimball, would always excuse himself after dinner to lie down for a few minutes. He never was shy about needing this time for recuperation. Since my retirement, I have often enjoyed a little power nap after lunch. It feels very natural.

Of course, sleep in general is very, very important. Many folks in this hectic age, no doubt, do not get enough sleep. And it's during sleep that the etheric body does its energizing work of repairing and enlivening the physical cells. In the medical chapter, I spoke about how the etheric body has the tendency to expand, while the astral forces contract and hold the energy in. During the sleep process, the personality in the astral sheath withdraws from the physical body (usually just a few feet away), and the etheric's expansive energies are thereby freed and released to restore physical tissue. After sleep, the astral reconnects, and the body wakes up refreshed.

People who snore or perhaps are a bit overweight, I feel, should be tested for sleep apnea. Sleep apnea is a condition in which the breathing airways become restricted, and the lack of oxygen wakes up a person in order to take in a deep breath. People with severe sleep apnea can wake up sometimes eighty times an hour. Now imagine the astral body withdrawing from the physical as the sleep process begins. Every time the person wakes up, the astral has to re-enter the physical. The astral body of people with sleep apnea bounce back and forth like a yo-yo. And the etheric forces are never released long enough to have the really restorative effect on the physical cells. Physical health problems are the result, along with chronic tiredness.

Beyond the sleep issue, I have personally found many other ways to rejuvenate my energy system when necessary. Of course, the most obvious way is through diet and nutrition. There's only one trouble with discussing nutrition: I've found that despite nutritional experts saying otherwise, it's virtually impossible to lay down any helpful guidelines that apply to everyone. In a real sense, "one man's meat is another man's poison." I, for instance, have been an ovo-lacto vegetarian for fifty years, and I operate very well on this diet. Hana, on the other hand, needs to eat meat to keep her energy rolling. The best explanation I have read for this type of variation in dietary needs is the "blood type" diet. According to this philosophy, my wife's blood type O needs to have meat, while my type A positive does very well on a vegetarian diet. Type A's also like coffee and red wine, which is true in my case. Speaking of coffee and psychic energy: Rudolf Steiner remarked that coffee stimulates logical thinking, while tea brings out a social response in people. I have a cup of coffee by my side as I write these lines.

Another way to stimulate or change energy patterns is by becoming mindful of the breath. The Sufis say that God is closer to you than your own breath. But that also implies that breath is about as close to your life energy as you can get. In the East, breathing exercises to bring prana (or life energy from the subtle planes) into your consciousness are very common in the practice of various forms of yoga. In the West, however, elaborate breathing exercises can become problematic. When Meher Baba reoriented Inayat Khan's Sufi school in the West, he eliminated many breathing exercises that were not necessary for Westerners and included only one simple breath exercise in the Sufi charter he wrote. Generally, simply being mindful of the breath moving in and out of your body can be a helpful process. You will find that such mindfulness calms the nervous system and centers vital energy.

I can give two examples of using a breath exercise from the same day. I had just gotten news that I owed way more income tax than I was counting on. I was feeling down and decided to take my dog for a walk in downtown Walnut Creek. I sat down by a fountain and focused on my breath, trying to synchronize with inhalations and exhalations with my Master's name. I not only felt more chipper after a few minutes of mindful breathing, but the thought came out of the blue that it was my puppy's birthday that day. My entire mood shifted.

Later that same day, after eating lunch, I was preparing to go to a school to teach dance and singing games to the second graders. I thought I might have a quick power nap to prepare for the class. However, spinning in my mind were all the songs and tunes I needed to use for my dance class. I couldn't relax. I started my mindful breathing practice, my mind immediately got still, and I was able to have a short, reviving rest.

Another way to enliven drooping energies is to have a good aerobic exercise session. I like to have a half-hour swim. For this Pisces, it's easy to get motivated to jump into a swimming pool. For others, a brisk walk is the best energizing technique. Of course, a walk in a natural setting is best. The firm earth beneath your feet and trees and grass and flowers and animals all around you is a perfect setting for boosting energy. Pachamama, the name the Andean Indians call Mother Earth, is always ready and eager to offer nurturance. Sunlight is also healing. It is said that walking or sitting in the sunshine on a cold day can chase away the winter blues.

These few comments on the energy structure within human beings only barely scratch the surface of all that could be said. But any greater awareness of the hidden side of life can make life more happy, healthy, and interesting. In addition, these insights are also very practical and can even be transformative.

CONCLUSION

One of humankind's abiding obsessions throughout the ages has been the search for spiritual truths. Is there a spiritual world? How can you connect with it? Is there a god, and how can you find him (or her)? Mystics have reported seeing God everywhere and in everything. Psychic mediums have reported that the spiritual world of discarnate beings, even some relatives, is all around us continually.

For me, the most practical way to put descendant spirituality into practice in my daily life is to become more mindful and aware of the omnipresent reality of the sea of unseen energies always at work in us and around us. The Mother of the Sri Aurobindo ashram calls this mindfulness being conscious of the "dance of vibrations."

> We live unawares in an enormous vortex of billions and trillions of vibrations. All the time one is vibrating in response to vibrations which come from outside. If [only] you could see the kind of dance, the dance of the vibrations which is there around you all the time. (Georges Van Vrekhem, *The Mother*, 2012, p 471)

The Hidden Side of Life has described ways of becoming aware of this "dance of vibrations" in practical aspects of life: in medicine, gardening, child-rearing, and so on. Meher Baba once said, "The most practical thing to be in the world is to be spiritually minded." Cultivating an intuitive awareness of these inner energies affecting us every second is a fun way to become more "spiritually minded." My son, Blake, objects to me calling this spiritual awareness "fun." But why not? At times, the everyday routines of life and the continual burden of responsibilities can make life feel difficult. Not only can mindfulness of energies bring zest into your life, but you can also learn to channel these forces into a more healthful and energetic lifestyle. I've just started drinking water from copper cups, for example. Dr. Rudolf Steiner always used to say copper stimulated the blood and the flow of etheric energy in your health aura. Also, I learned on the internet that copper-charged water heals and strengthens the liver.

As I was talking to Hana about concluding my book, she casually mentioned, "Did I ever tell you about my experience on the kitchen floor in high school?" She then went on to describe this experience: "When I was in high school, one day I was talking on the phone in our kitchen. I was sitting cross-legged on the kitchen floor. All of a sudden, everything around me became a sea of energy. Nothing was solid to my vision. The energy was movement and vortexes of color. My cat walked by me, and rather than being solid, she was simply moving colors, moving energy. The energies continually changed and swirled. Then, as suddenly as the experience started, everything was back to normal."

But the reality was that everything was not back to normal. It was only Hana's vision that slipped back. The world around her still vibrated as a "sea of energy," sustaining life in every way imaginable.

David Spangler mentions in the chapter on the mineral kingdom that we should try to enhance our "energy sense" in order to be more conscious of the flowing energies around us. To be aware of energies, we need a healthy and vibrant etheric body. There are many ways to ensure this: breathing pure air, getting regular exercise, eating nutritious food, and drinking plenty of water. Also essential are keeping your environment clean, meditating daily, taking frequent trips into nature, and nurturing loving friendships with folks with like-minded ideas. Finally, you can bolster the energies circulating in the etheric realm by exhibiting a cheerful and optimistic attitude towards the vicissitudes of life.

The Mother of the Sri Aurobindo ashram also speaks about collaborating with the forces of the inner dimensions. Collaboration means not controlling these energies, but rather blending with them: going with the flow. Such collaboration can lead to a life of love and happiness.

Printed in the United States
by Baker & Taylor Publisher Services